She Sat Where They Sat

Christian World Mission Books

Richard H. Drummond, *A History of Christianity in Japan*
Justo L. Gonzalez, *The Development of Christianity in the Latin Caribbean*
Stephen Neill, *The Story of the Christian Church in India and Pakistan*
Jane M. Sales, *The Planting of the Churches in South Africa*

R. Pierce Beaver, *All Loves Excelling*
Elizabeth Kelsey Kinnear, *She Sat Where They Sat: A Memoir of Anna Young Thompson*

Kenneth Strachan, *The Inescapable Calling*

William J. Danker, *Profit for the Lord*
A. Theodore Eastman, *Chosen and Sent: Calling the Church to Mission*
Donald C. Lord, *Mo Bradley and Thailand*
Paul B. Pedersen, *Batak Blood and Protestant Soul: The Development of National Batak Churches in North Sumatra*
David M. Stowe, *Ecumenicity and Evangelism*

R. Pierce Beaver, *To Advance the Gospel: The Collected Writings of Rufus Anderson*
R. Pierce Beaver, *Pioneers in Mission*
James A. Scherer, *Justinian Welz: Essays by an Early Prophet of Mission*
Max A. C. Warren, *To Apply the Gospel: Selections from the Writings of Henry Venn*

She Sat Where They Sat

A Memoir of Anna Young Thompson of Egypt

by

ELIZABETH KELSEY KINNEAR

WILLIAM B. EERDMANS PUBLISHING COMPANY
GRAND RAPIDS, MICHIGAN

TO MY HUSBAND, JIM
who endured many long, silent evenings
while this book was in progress

EDITORIAL FOREWORD

It may today seem incredible that the highest deliberative body in any American denomination would appoint a young woman to be a missionary overseas without first having raised the question with her. Yet this actually happened at a time when mission boards were still reluctant to send forth unmarried women and when the first separate women's boards were being founded expressly for that purpose. That young woman of twenty years was a pioneer among single women missionaries in general. She made no claim to fame or to unusual competence and achievement; but her achievement was prodigious in manifold forms of ministry throughout a long lifetime. She loved her Lord and she loved persons for his sake. The circumstances of living and working in a national capital and an Islamic state make some aspects of Miss Thompson's story different from that of single women missionaries elsewhere, but she is a typical and worthy representative of that whole glorious company of pioneers.

Mrs. Elizabeth K. Kinnear's memoir of Anna Y. Thompson is a book in the series, "Women in Mission," which in turn is a division of *Christian World Mission Books*. This library of paperback volumes is ecumenical in scope and authorship, and it deals with history, theory, methods, functional ministries, regional studies, biography, and source material — the entire range of the study of world mission.

—R. Pierce Beaver
Editor

CONTENTS

FOREWORD

This story was drawn from personal recollections, from the *Triennial Reports* and other records of the American Mission in Egypt filed with the Missionary Research Library at Union Theological Seminary in New York City, from *Minutes* of the General Assembly of the United Presbyterian Church of North America, from microfilmed *Minutes* of the Egyptian Presbytery and the Mission Association meetings, from the first forty-six volumes of the *Women's Missionary Magazine* (U.P.N.A.), and especially from Miss Thompson's papers and diaries covering many years of her life in Egypt. These are now in the care of the Presbyterian Historical Society in Philadelphia. Letters to more than thirty of Miss Thompson's former colleagues, American and Egyptian, brought so many kind replies that it is impossible to list all of the names. However, I must express here my appreciation of this generous sharing of their memories of a remarkable woman and a devoted missionary.

—E.K.K.

Miss Anna Y. Thompson—Egypt—1920

CHAPTER I

THE MAKING OF A MISSIONARY

In the early morning of a November day in 1871 a tall, soberly dressed young woman moved about her room in a New York home, gathering up her belongings. In a few minutes she would be leaving for the docks to board the steamer *Abyssinia,* beginning a journey of over six thousand miles with strangers. In another room of the house a man picked up a pencil and hurriedly wrote a farewell note. It read in part:

"My dear Sister: It is in some respects a time of trial for you. In a few hours you will probably feel more alone and lonely than you have ever felt in your life. . . . Feel that Jesus once went on the same errand on which you now go and He will not let you go alone. . . . Tell Him all your heart's wishes and sorrow and loneliness and need, and one whisper of His voice, 'Lo, I am with thee,' will make up for everything. Every day read some in His word. Cultivate Christian acquaintances. Take the opportunity if it at all occurs, even on shipboard or anywhere, to speak a private, earnest loving word for your Saviour.

"Try to see and feel as little as possible of the little inconveniences and annoyances of life in everyday matters, and think of the greater mercies and blessings you enjoy and which infinitely outweigh these. . . . This will sweeten many bitter hours of life.

"Our acquaintance has been very pleasant. You are leaving behind many who have learned to love you. You will often be earnestly prayed for. Write and you will always and fully be answered. And now, my Sister—may God bless you. Mizpah."

It was signed by Dr. J. B. Dales, secretary of the Foreign Mission Board of the United Presbyterian Church. A great many years later the little note, very creased, worn by handling, and obviously much treasured, was entrusted to a woman on the newer Women's Board of the United Presbyterian Church. It had belonged to Anna Y. Thompson, one of the pioneer women missionaries to Egypt. She was only twenty years old the day she received it, but she lived to serve sixty-one years on the field and became probably the best known woman in the valley of the Nile. To those who knew her during that long life, the precious little letter reads like her personal creed.

Miss Thompson came from a deeply religious family. Her father, David Thompson, was born in Ireland but came to live with relatives in Pennsylvania as a young boy. After his graduation from college and theological seminary he became pastor of a church known as Mt. Hope. There he married Rachel Lee from near Canonsburg, Pennsylvania. Anna, their youngest child, was born on March 11, 1851, when her parents were living at Bavington with the Robinson congregation. Family records show that the baby girl was baptized "Nancy Lee," but "Nancy" quickly became "Anna" and she herself adopted the second name of "Young" when she was in her teens. In later years in the mission circle she was affectionately known as "Miss Anna Y."

In 1853 Dr. Thompson started overland with his family and a company of friends to the Willamette Valley of Oregon. They traveled by train, river steamer, and covered wagon. As they were crossing the Missouri River, their steamer was involved in an accident. Although all of the party were able to go on, Anna's mother later succumbed to the effects of the accident, dying of pneumonia as they were crossing the plains of Nebraska. After her burial the sad family and friends drove the wagons back and forth over the lonely spot in order to make sure the Indians would not notice the disturbed ground and open the grave. An uncle, Hugh Lee, and his wife undertook the care of the five children.

Anna was eight years old when her father moved the family East again. They traveled by ship from Portland to San Francisco and then on south to the isthmus of Panama. Since this of course antedated the digging of the Canal, Anna remembered vividly their

ride across the isthmus. From there they took ship again to
Philadelphia.

The Thompson family was broken up once more after reaching
Pennsylvania. Anna was left with Mr. William Young and his sisters,
members of the Sixth United Presbyterian Church in Philadelphia,
and a very devout family. It was gratitude for their loving care that
moved Anna to take "Young" as a middle name.

In 1859 Dr. Thompson married Miss Margaret Burnside and
gathered up his family again. They moved to the Clear Fork
congregation in Guernsey County, Ohio. Anna was living in this
home at Milnersville when she was appointed to go to Egypt, and
those church ties remained close all during her missionary service.
The women of her father's presbytery of Muskingum helped to
support her from 1886, and from 1892 they undertook the whole of
her salary. (The amount does not seem munificent by today's
standards—a $200 outfit allowance, not repeated, and $500 a year
for the salary of an unmarried woman missionary. A single man did a
little better with a $300 outfit allowance and $800 a year salary.)

Miss Thompson's name has always been closely associated with
the First Ohio presbytery as well, and there are many missionary
societies and circles in the United Presbyterian congregations that
still carry her name. She was made a life director of the Women's
General Missionary Society in 1930, one of a noble band supported
by a mission board that had great difficulty being born. The
women's request for a charter was ignored or rejected many times by
the General Assembly of the denomination, but even before the
women had official sanction, the Foreign Mission Board had enough
faith in them to ask that they support ten foreign workers. By 1916
there were still ten women in active service who had gone to the
fields of Egypt and India in the years 1871-1886, and Anna Y.
Thompson led the list.

The story of Miss Thompson's appointment to the work in Egypt
was an unusual one. Fifty years later, when some newly arrived
missionaries heard it, they reacted in stupefied amazement.

"They actually appointed you when you'd never *applied?* They
didn't even ask you if you were interested?" they asked in shocked
voices. "Surely you should have been *consulted!*"

Miss Thompson did not agree. "I was honored to be selected by
the highest court of the church," she answered. "I didn't know for
many years who had suggested my name, or who the others were

who sponsored me, but my father approved, and I could only accept it as God's will for me." She felt no resentment at what the younger missionaries considered a very highhanded procedure. On the contrary, this was one of her proudest memories.

The General Assembly's minutes reported that at their meeting in Xenia, Ohio, they chose eight young people for mission service. At the next meeting in Washington, Iowa, in July, 1872, the minutes report that of the eight, only Miss Thompson accepted. The record reads, "The last Assembly, with great solemnity and unanimity appointed eight new persons to our respective missions. Much consultation and prayer in consideration of the whole subject followed." Apparently they decided that more consultation and prayer were needed, for that was the last time such a procedure was followed. The Foreign Board had expressed its concern to the Assembly about this method of appointment, feeling that more caution was advisable. They wrote, "Before putting any young man in such a position it ought to be well known that he has been consulted, or at least that there is no insuperable barrier to his going, if he should be appointed."

Looking back to those days on her twenty-first birthday, already busy with her mission work, Anna wrote:

"In some ways I am such a child, and my past life has seemed so short. This time last year I was a school girl at the seminary. Our missionary to China visited Washington and I became much interested in the cause of missions. At the suggestion of Mrs. Hanna (head of the seminary) I thought it was my duty to go to China. Accordingly I went home to see if my father would give consent. He did not see it to be my duty to go—he preferred Egypt or India, but would not say nay if he thought it was the Lord's will. He suggested I go South to teach the colored folks, and I then became interested in them. I went to Mrs. Hanna and when she spoke favorably of the plan, I immediately wrote asking for an appointment, but was told all positions were occupied. Mrs. Hanna said she was glad, as others would do for the South, and she thought favorably of my going to teach in Salinas Valley in California. Having obtained father's consent, I wrote there, but a reply was received that all the schools were engaged. I felt perfectly willing, knowing that where there was no opening for me it was not the will of the Lord for me to go. We concluded I should return to the seminary for another year, but that evening I heard that I had been appointed missionary to Egypt. It was quite a surprise to me as I had given up the notion of going any place for a few years. However, I immediately thought it was a call of Providence and decided to go if father would consent."

All of this was happening while Anna was still preparing for her examinations at the famous Female Seminary in Washington, Pennsylvania, where both she and her sister were students. The examinations in Literature, Bible Dictionary and Moral Science were successfully passed, and Anna went home to prepare for her great adventure. On the day the seminary closed she had received an offer of a teaching position in a school where she had served the previous summer, but this she refused without hesitation. It amused her that she seemed suddenly to have become a person of some status. She wrote, "Some people were kinder to me and treated me as if I were of more importance."

The next few weeks were spent in visiting friends and in preparation for her departure. When it came time for her to travel to New York with her father, the home church gave her a fine send-off. She was completely astonished to see that some of the people cared enough about her leaving to weep.

On a dark, foggy morning they had family prayers and then started off to Cambridge in a spring wagon, reaching the railway station about seven. The pastor of the Cambridge United Presbyterian Church came with his wife to see her off. There were no tears on Anna's part until they steamed out of Pittsburgh when the reality of her leaving home swept over her. But a young man on the train, learning the purpose of her journey, started an argument about the relative importance of home and foreign missions. Soon the eager young missionary found herself too busy holding up her end of the discussion to indulge in self-pity. They made a lengthy stop in Washington and Anna was invited to stay in her old room in the seminary. Mrs. Hanna was very kind to her, giving her a gift of money and her loving blessing. There was some final shopping in Philadelphia, where they spent several days in Dr. Dales' home.

The young woman and the distinguished minister were like-minded, and quickly became friends. Anna wrote later, "He looked so kind and spoke so tenderly to me that I immediately loved him. And here commenced a friendship which I hope nothing but death shall sever, and if I survive him I shall certainly revere his memory." (The friendship did indeed last until Dr. Dales' death in 1893.) Anna reported later, "Dr. Dales was much concerned lest I should ever regret my choice. In other words, that I would not always be satisfied with a single life. I told him that I had always led a quiet life, had never allowed myself to be carried away in love matters, and that I had been used to little attentions from gentlemen and not indulged in novel reading; that if ever I should change my views I would tell him." The day would come when Anna would change her mind, but her advisers then were less sympathetic than this old friend.

After a brief stay in New York the great day of departure arrived. Dr. Dales and Dr. Thompson escorted Anna to the boat, where she joined her traveling companions, the Galbreaths and Miss Dodds, Covenanter missionaries on their way to Syria. Dr. Thompson found the separation very painful, breaking down completely and weeping aloud. He begged Anna to forgive him as he had not always done his duty to her or any of his children. This sentiment, however, was not shared by his daughter, then or ever.

The tension was broken by an interruption. One of the boat's officers had been impressed by the handsome young woman just come aboard and he was asking for an introduction. Anna's father immediately took alarm. He warned her solemnly to be careful about such men, and told her she was likely to err by being too free!

By evening, when the partings were past and the boat was well out to sea, the little group started to sing. This was something Anna loved, although she admitted that it sometimes made her feel sad. One of the passengers pretended not to enjoy this pastime. One evening he inquired whether it was Anna who was doing the "howling." It was not long until she had become the lively center of the group. She admitted to being an "everlasting talker" and soon carried nearly half of the conversation. When the Sabbath arrived and the passengers asked for some music, young Miss Thompson insisted that it would have to be a Psalm. She was staunchly backed by her Covenanter friends, but the rest of the party said they were great bigots and would certainly change their views during the next twenty years. Probably Miss Thompson had as much to do with making the Egyptian Protestant Church a Psalm-singing church as anyone, but that is a long story and deserves special mention later.

The party disembarked in Liverpool and went to stay at a temperance hotel. Anna said that since she was the *largest* of the company and a talker, they made her sit at the head of the table and most of the time it fell to her to order the meals. They were to take the *Hector* from Liverpool, but in their ignorance of the docks and the indifference of the cab driver they almost boarded a boat named *Marathon* at an entirely different dock. After some excitement and a great rush they located their own boat and started on the second leg of the long journey. Anna took her full share of teasing from the older men on board. At Gibraltar the signal flags were hoisted and were interpreted for her as saying that there were fourteen passengers aboard, one a young, *tall* one. (One signal flag happened to be a very long one.) Actually, a report was being sent to Lloyd's of London.

On December 7 the boat arrived in Alexandria. Miss Thompson wrote that she then resolved to like the country and "though having a dread of ophthalmia" (with very good reason in those days) "I thought I would try to be happy and contented as I always have been, as my sister said." Dr. David Strang came to meet the newcomer and she almost lost her self-possession, being suddenly overcome with embarrassment and fear that the missionaries would be disappointed in her. But she soon felt at home, drinking in all the new sights and sounds with unusual keenness. She even tried on those first days to write down the tunes of the street calls and the children's street games in the sol-fa notation.

After a week, she went on to Cairo where she was met by another of the mission staff, Dr. Gulian Lansing, a man who was to play a surprising and enigmatic part in her later life. Fifty years later Miss Thompson remembered that Dr. Lansing's sermon on her first Sunday was on the text, "The Lord is good; a stronghold in the day of trouble." There were three missionary couples and one single woman missionary then living in the old mission house, which had been obtained from the government under the Viceroy Said Pacha. (Later this building was exchanged for land for the one still in use in the Ezbekieh section of Cairo. It stands opposite the site of the former well-known Shepheard's Hotel, burned in the riots of 1952.) In addition to the residences, Miss Thompson found a boys' school and a church in the mission building.

Like any newcomer to Egypt, Anna spent her second day in Cairo on a trip to the pyramids in Giza. The party went inside and she complained, "The passages are so low and I am so tall!" A few days later three of the mission wives took her to see the school in Haret es Sakkain, the Street of the Water Carriers. This was her first attempt to ride a donkey and she found it very funny until the return journey, when the donkey, like so many of its Egyptian peers, stumbled and went down abruptly onto its knees, giving her a humiliating fall.

On the 22nd of December Anna went to visit her cousin, Henrietta Harvey, and her husband, Dr. William Harvey, whom she was meeting for the first time. Their mission station was Sinnoris in the oasis of Fayoum, several hours by train from Cairo and across the desert from Wasta. Christmas Day marked the beginning of Anna's regular study of Arabic with a teacher, but she proudly announced that she already knew thirty words. A later teacher in Mansura complimented her on her pronunciation, except for the difficult consonant "ain" which is the downfall of so many aspiring Western linguists. Anna's friends told her she learned fast because she talked all the time and wasn't afraid of making mistakes.

Though she was studying hard, mainly in the Gospel of John, Anna frequently went out calling with Mrs. Harvey. She was an object of the greatest curiosity to the village women, who were not used to single women if they were neither blind nor crippled. They asked Mrs. Harvey, "Why does such a good-looking girl not get married? We suppose a hundred Napoleons would not buy her!" Anna commented, "I suppose they were right." On the same walk they met a small girl, perhaps five years old, who was wearing nothing but brass earrings and bracelets. Anna said, "That seemed to me was not enough to cover her nakedness."

Sometimes it was annoying and a little frightening to be the object of so much curiosity as the ladies aroused. One evening they saw some fresh cucumbers on sale at the edge of an open market, but as soon as they stopped·to buy some, people began to gather. Dr. Harvey and the Egyptian teacher immediately joined them, but crowds began running from all directions, and others rushed to doors and housetops to see what was going on. When Anna and the Harveys reached the edge of the town they were struck by the beauty of the evening, and stopped to look. Anna wrote, "A most magnificent scene met our eyes,—the threshing floor in abundance near us, the beautiful country, the flocks and herds coming home, the groves of palms, the distant lake, the smoking sugar factory, and the background of hills and cloudless sky, all lit up with the glory of the setting sun. But grand as this was, we could not resist the temptation to look back at our followers and to laugh at how terrified they became when Dr. Harvey began to count them. But the crowd increased and it became annoying as they made such a dust." Finally Dr. Harvey turned and waved his cane threateningly and most of them ran away. There must have been a hundred of them, making it difficult to have an evening walk in comfort. Another new experience for the young missionary was her first meal in an Egyptian home. Since they were to attend a wedding in a few days' time, the head of the mission school, Hag Hanna, invited them to his house for dinner as a practice session for Miss Thompson. As she described it, "The dinner was on a little round table. There was a large turkey in the middle, soup dishes with meat and onions boiled together and bread cut in pieces all around, some cheese, boiled rice and apricots. After Mr. Harvey asked a blessing the guests commenced by pushing up their sleeves and looking very business-like. Then Henrietta said, 'Who will carve the turkey?' and she took it, as is the style, and broke or pulled it to pieces with her hands. It was very nice and tender and was stuffed with rice, raisins and hazel nuts. The meat was eaten with our fingers and the stuffing with wooden spoons. Hag Hanna took off some of the fat part of the breast and distributed it. I suppose from this that it is a choice part." (This will remind Miss Anna Y's old friends that it became her custom to place on an honored guest's plate a special tidbit from her own serving, to the open-mouthed astonishment of the visitor—if not a local person—and the blushing embarrassment of new missionaries who saw the performance as a shocking breach of good table manners. Miss Thompson always waited smilingly for the guest to acknowledge her thoughtful gesture, which had become entirely natural to her.) "Next came the rice and afterwards the mishmish (apricots). We washed our hands in the usual style by having water poured over them. This is very nice and refreshing. None of the women of the house were to be seen, except a sister-in-law, a widow."

In a few weeks Miss Thompson returned to Cairo and threw herself into language study with enthusiasm. On her twenty-first birthday there were no special celebrations, but in the evening, on her colleague Miss Eliza Johnston's invitation, she joined her for some singing. Soon another singer arrived, a visitor from Wales, so it was a happy evening after all for a young woman attaining her majority far from home and family. One of the mission wives had asked Anna that afternoon to read to her from a new biography of Henry Martyn. Her private comment later was that he "was certainly a pious man, but I could not help thinking how much better it would have been if he had taken that lady along with him as his wife. He must have suffered greatly when parting with friends."

Anna's Arabic teacher at this time was a lad of thirteen and she found him rather too easy on her, compared to the strictness of Hag Hanna in Sinnoris. One day, when she felt she was reading well, the young teacher allowed her to move on into the next chapter of John. Attacking it with self-confidence, she soon found she was making a great many ridiculous mistakes. This set her to laughing so that she was glad when the hour was up. It didn't take much to make the young Miss Thompson laugh, for she saw the humor in most situations. Sometimes this was embarrassing. Once in the early days she found the proceedings at a local wedding so unbearably funny that it was hard not to show that she was inwardly convulsed, and so insult her hosts. One of the British visitors to the mission told the young missionary that after staying in Egypt for a time she would "get sobered down." This, too, amused her. But she admitted that when she had worked hard on her Arabic lesson and it went badly, she often could not keep the tears back. Usually the Arabic lesson was a very serious matter to her.

The word got around that the new missionary was musical, so it was not long until the head of the boys' school in the mission building sent word that he would like her to teach the boys to sing. She found about sixty boys in the large room, well dressed, each wearing a red *tarboush.* She started them off with a Psalm sung to the tune "America." They sang rather harshly and flatted some of the notes, but by taking a seatful of boys at a time for practice, she soon had them making better music. Growing more ambitious, she wrote the scale on the board and drilled them on the notes. She was herself quick to pick up a new tune and she filled the margins of her notebooks with the songs she had heard, using the do-re-mi notation.

About this time she had her first glimpse of Dr. Andrew Watson from Mansura, the person whose plea for help had been responsible for her being appointed to Egypt. She said he was tall and fine looking, with dark hair and beard, and she had no doubt she would like him very much. At the April meeting of the mission association Dr. Watson said he was very anxious for a theological seminary to be opened and he suggested Mansura as the place for it. Somehow this brought up the matter of Miss Thompson's assignment. The Harveys would have been glad to have her with them in Sinnoris, but Dr. Watson said she had been sent out for Mansura. If she was sent anywhere else, he wanted the reasons assigned and recorded! This firm stand settled the matter, and Anna decided once again to be "contented and happy." Since it would be only a few weeks until most of the missionaries would be going to summer quarters, Dr. Watson told her she could choose whether to spend the time in Mansura or Sinnoris. She replied that she had come out expecting to do whatever the missionaries thought best, which Dr. Watson considered to be a very obedient attitude. It was decided that she should go to Sinnoris but see Mansura first.

It took courage for Anna to start off alone on her long day's journey to Mansura in the heart of the Delta. She could not converse well as yet and a change of trains was involved in the trip. All went well, however, and by five o'clock she was being welcomed by the Watsons at the Mansura station and taken to their home. She was pleased with the green countryside and the town, and happy with the missionaries.

The next day she visited the school she was to direct. There was no doubt she was needed. Dr. Watson had tried to keep the school open, although there was no really competent staff available. Anna found sixteen girls ranging in age from five to thirteen, not very well dressed and some not at all prepossessing. The single teacher was able neither to keep order nor to teach more than the alphabet and the first primer. After a short visit Mrs. Watson and the new headmistress went to take a look at the boys' school. Anna remarked that everywhere she had gone she had been impressed with the realization that the boys were brighter looking than the girls. Perhaps the reasons for this were not far to seek—parents in those days expected nothing from their daughters so far as their minds were concerned, and gave them little encouragement to improve themselves.

Anna did not lose a day in her language study, taking advantage of help from a young teacher who served as Dr. Watson's secretary. When she listened to Dr. Watson's account of how he had slaved over the language, she felt a little discouraged at the prospect, thinking she was not working hard enough. But when she learned about his terrible suffering with ophthalmia, she decided there was reason not to overdo it. Her second lesson with this most particular teacher was a trial. He forced her to try over and over again to pronounce the word *surirak* (your bed) until she was in despair, not being able to hear what she was doing wrong. When he shook his head and gave up, she fled into the study and burst into tears. Trying to understand her own behavior later, she decided she must be very dull and ought to have studied more, or perhaps her teacher in Cairo should have been more particular with her. Afterwards Dr. Watson helped her read some in the Gospel of Mark. She understood why the people said he spoke like an Egyptian, and she decided his Scotch accent was a help!

The Watsons planned a river expedition for the next day and set off in good time, supplied with shawls and lunch basket. The wind filled the big sails and kept them moving at a good pace. Dr. Watson thought it would be more romantic to eat on the river bank under a long avenue of sycamore and willow trees, so they left the boat for their meal and a walk. The group made a call in the small town that had been their goal, and about the middle of the afternoon they started back to Mansura. A smart breeze was now against them. The boatmen had to pull the boat by a rope from the shore for a time, then try to row back and forth, gaining a little each time. The sun set and the moon came up while they still struggled to make headway. But now the boatmen began to brighten their task by singing a repetitive, extempore chant about the day's happenings. Anna described their song as unmusical and sometimes senseless, but there was something romantic about it. She searched for a scrap of paper to note down the tune, but there was none to be had. However, Miss Thompson was not so easily balked—she wrote it on her handkerchief!

Dr. Watson had no illusions about the difficulties to be faced by missionaries in the Mansura area. He was convinced the school would pick up if "good order were kept." But more than once he himself, devoted missionary that he was, felt he must give up. He wrote in 1873, "Sometimes we have thought that we have not the proper qualifications for this field; sometimes that the Lord has no chosen ones here; sometimes that He desires us to go to another town. . . . Yet the Master has not left us without some tokens of His favor." He had been happy about Anna Thompson's appointment and sent word home when she arrived. "It is with pleasure that I mention the arrival of Miss Anna Y. Thompson in Egypt, in response to the request in my last report. She is greatly needed, and we hope and pray that the Master may bless her labors for the eternal happiness of some of her Egyptian sisters now in such a deplorable state of ignorance, sin and spiritual death."

But more Arabic was needed before effective work could be done, and Miss Thompson went back to that grueling task, staying with the Harveys in Sinnoris. She admitted that people were in and out of the house every minute of the day, and this was probably a distraction from the Arabic but very interesting and enlightening for the newcomer. By the time the hot weather arrived her fears about ophthalmia seemed to be coming to pass. The Harvey baby also had sore eyes so the household left for Cairo, with Anna not expecting to return to Sinnoris.

On reaching Ramleh, the summer home of the mission people, she met Dr. and Mrs. John Hogg from Assiut. They amused her by deciding that she had a cast of features like ancient Egyptian faces—that her eyes especially were like those of the painted ones of pharaonic women. The pictures we have of Anna at this time show a person of natural dignity, quietly dressed, with broad brow and regular features. The demure outward appearance disguised a personality of rare sensitivity and real humor. One of her closest friends later described her as being full of "charm and quaint surprises." Now the time had come for the first real test of her missionary vocation. Anna Thompson was headmistress of the American mission's girls' school in the provincial city of Mansura.

CHAPTER II

NEW HOPE FOR SOME OF EGYPT'S GIRLS

The Mansura school opened in October with twenty-some girls, of all ages and categories. Anna's efforts to classify them convinced her that each one would have to be tutored individually for a while. Dr. Watson came in each morning to open the day with prayers and give the girls a little talk, to which they listened very politely. Miss Thompson discovered that the previous teacher had little good to say for her charges, reporting that one was an *afrit* (little devil) and others were crazy! The children very obviously had been having their own way most of the time. The schoolroom was pleasant, with a magnificent view of the river and the fields beyond, but there was little opportunity to enjoy it. Finally the new head had the students assigned to suitable tasks, with one of the older girls responsible for each of the younger ones. The schedule was rather like that of a one-room schoolhouse in the States. Teaching materials were quite different, however. The reading lessons were all in the Arabic New Testament and the singing lesson was Psalm 37.

Some of the mixed Egyptian and European families in the town were concerned that their daughters should learn French and would have brought them to the mission school if Anna had been able to teach that language. She contented herself with trying a little English with the more advanced pupils.

Soon she also undertook to teach two or three of the women how to read, while she kept up her own study of Arabic several hours a day. Callers to the mission household brought her some interesting sidelights on human nature. One evening, when a small group of women were mutually accusing each other of telling tales, they were sternly lectured on forgiveness by Mrs. Watson. Anna reported that the discussion became warm and she grew so interested that she "came near having a headache over it."

Usually when she attended the Arabic church service a former monk was the preacher. He had studied some Bible fragments which were available to him in the monastery as a young man. One day a man arrived from Cairo with a whole Bible. *Abuna* (Father) Michael traded a pair of new red shoes for the Bible and studied it diligently. Eventually he left the monastery and went to Alexandria. There he married and later was ordained as the first Protestant Egyptian minister. He was a longtime colleague of Miss Thompson in the Bulak area in Cairo and always called her his cousin—"daughter of my uncle."

Word came from the States that a new single missionary had been appointed, and Anna and Mrs. Watson wrote to invite her to visit them in Mansura. It was Miss Margaret (Maggie) Smith, who was to be Miss Thompson's fellow worker for the next sixty years. Anna liked her on sight, saying she was "very small, with very long, light hair, very humble and unpretending." The tiny woman's great crown of hair was her only vanity. It hung almost to her knees and was never cut. As for being humble, she was also indomitable, as Miss Thompson and others learned in the years ahead. As a girl, Miss Smith had crossed the country in a covered wagon train led by her father, a United Presbyterian minister. The group founded a new town in Kansas and lived through some very hard days. Whatever the source of her courage, little Miss Smith completely intimidated some difficult and angry men during her missionary career. While she was head of the girls' orphanage in Cairo, one determined father tried to take his ten-year-old daughter away to marry her off. Miss Smith spoke to him so sternly that he put off the wedding for two years. In telling others about it he said, *"Ya salaam!"* (Oh peace!—an expression of surprise) "That little woman's words affected me so that the hairs of my head stood on end, and the perspiration ran down my spine!"

After Miss Smith had completed her visit and gone away to begin her language study, Anna worked hard to improve the school's routine and added several more women to her list of private pupils. Some of them proved to be disappointments, but others had less opposition from their husbands and struggled along with the difficult task. It was always a trial to Anna to sit down in disordered and dirty rooms, but this was very often a thing she had to do. She said that one home was so filthy that the previous missionary always went home from a visit there violently ill. It was their custom to bring a small table or stool for the visitor to sit on, putting a towel or something over it. One day the man of the house, not seeing anything else handy, took off his headkerchief and spread it for her with great formality. She admitted that the chickens in the room bothered her a good deal too.

At the presbytery meeting in April it was decided that the Watsons should be transferred to Cairo, and this saddened the little group of church members in Mansura very much. Dr. and Mrs. D. R. Johnston joined Miss Thompson for the next two or three months, and she felt that the school was going well. A solid morning of lessons was followed by a break for lunch and then she went back to help the girls with sewing and writing. The attendance was up to about fifty. Her own Arabic lessons continued, along with the reading lessons for the women and a Bible class on Sabbath afternoons.

A little break in the heavy schedule came in May when she was asked to join a party making a trip to Suez. It was during that trip that she had her first experience in riding a camel, and this should be reported in her own words:

"I pushed my right foot over and was soon seated as proudly as you please on this ship of the desert, and called lustily to Mrs. Johnston to get on. Reluctantly she mounted the back of the bended Bedouin and was soon seated in front of me astride and both of us laughing immoderately. . . . So we jogged along until I thought 'Oh for a stirrup in which to rest my long legs which were grinning miserably far below the borders of my dress, and I was unable to raise my foot or lower my dress over it. . . . [As they stopped] the camel gave a jolting pitch down onto its knees which was almost too much for us . . . then down it went, back onto its hind knees, then a shake, a settle, then a final getting onto its breast and another shake and settling—all the time groaning and growling with anger."

As the hot weather increased their discomfort, the strain of Anna's work began to tell on her health, and it was decided that they must get down to the seashore. She had been pleased with the girls' progress, saying they deserved credit for their diligence and general behavior. She wrote, "The girls commit Scripture with readiness and sing with spirit and delight." This sentence holds the key to two of Miss Thompson's lifelong interests—the study of the Bible and the joy of music. She had much to do with the preparation of the first Arabic psalter for the Egyptian church, as was intimated earlier. She also kept up interest in the memorization of the Bible, securing a fund for special prizes of Bibles for hundreds of Egyptian young people.

The Johnstons' assignment to Mansura had been only temporary. Now all the staff was needed elsewhere and Anna was faced with the task of closing the school. She could not keep back the tears as she led in prayer for the last time with the girls. She realized she was still only a beginner in the language, but she hoped her labors had not been in vain. She prayed that the Lord would send more worthy laborers, but no one was available. Because of the shortage of workers, this school remained closed until Miss Galloway of the Associate Reformed Church arrived to take charge several years later.

All of Anna's newly gained experience was called into action the following September when she arrived in Sinnoris to take over the school there. When that school was in running order, after about three weeks, she also took charge of a second school in Medinet el Fayoum. This meant spending a full day in that city once a week. The traveling, four hours each way, had to be done on foot or on donkeyback. Often they were caught on the road by darkness. Miss Thompson carried a small folding lantern with literally one candle power. This was found among her possessions after her death and has become a part of the collection in the United Presbyterian Historical Society in Philadelphia.

The next months were valuable to the young missionary. She missed no chance to learn to be a real woman of the country, getting used to the people's ways and accommodating herself to whatever circumstances arose. At one time Mrs. Harvey joined her in Medina for four days' calling in the homes. After this a regular weekly prayer meeting was begun and nothing was allowed to interfere with it. Attendance was down one day because there had been a call for soldiers. Most of the townspeople locked their doors and went into hiding. The school servant was rounded up, his top knot was cut, and he was marched away.

In addition to her work in the villages of the oasis, Anna

sometimes traveled with the Harveys and others on the mission *dahabiya* or houseboat, to places along the river not otherwise accessible. The visitors always got a warm welcome, and services in the little churches were quickly arranged. These churches were usually dirt floored, with a wall or a curtain separating the men from the women. It was a common custom to drive a sheep through the room before a service on the theory that the usual assembly of fleas would go out with it. The missionaries were frequently doubtful of the efficacy of the practice, and with good reason. The children were very much in evidence, running back and forth between their parents on the two sides of the curtain, but their noise seemed not to cause the worshipers any concern. Sometimes a late arrival would walk with great dignity up the aisle and shake hands politely with the preacher, though he might be halfway through his sermon. This again caused no comment, since the man was simply showing his respect to the visitor.

The mission ladies were distressed at the dirty condition of the children, but realized that they lived in the dust and that every drop of water had to be carried from the river on the mothers' heads. The people, however poor, provided the best they had. Time meant little in the villages, so it was not unusual to wait for nearly two hours while a meal was being prepared, and Mrs. Harvey said, "It was none the worse for having to be eaten with our fingers." One small village had not yet succeeded in building a church, though they had settled upon a site and begun to make the sun-dried brick. The men sat in a room by themselves, but the only place for the women was the cow stable. They brought chairs for the mission women, but the village women and girls had to sit on the floor of the stable between the visitors and a big buffalo cow, which had no reverence for the occasion. Several other cows and two donkeys inhabited the adjoining room.

Some of the little churches did not have packed earthen floors and the men and women sat in three or four inches of dust. On one occasion a chair was brought for the missionary, but when he sat down he immediately sank into the dust and his knees rose until his position was too ludicrous to maintain. They rushed out and brought a large cotton cushion to restore his dignity. When he got up to talk, he was careful to stand with his nose exactly in line with the center partition so he could talk to both men and women. The open windows were full of noisy youngsters trying to see what was going on inside. One of the men would take a run around the building to chase them away, but by the time he reached the door again the windows would be as full as ever, with the fighting and the laughter renewed. As the scrambling outside and the crying of the babies inside grew louder, the missionary would stand on tiptoe and raise his voice higher and higher. It was more exhausting than fuuny at the time, and they wondered whether anyone had understood the message. But the people felt they were getting a blessing and always thanked the visitors very warmly and courteously for coming.

In February Miss Thompson had a very unusual adventure. A man in the town was building a new boat and he asked the missionaries to go out with his family and friends at the time of launching it on the large lake. Mrs. Harvey was not free to go when the date finally arrived, after three postponements. The Egyptian women helpers were anxious to go, so Miss Thompson, who admitted to being eager to see the lake, decided to accept the invitation if donkeys could be found for them. A group of about fifteen started off in single file. Anna enjoyed the fresh air and the sweet fragrance from the bean fields, but she was disappointed to see the way the people in the area were living. Only a few had mud-brick houses. Most families lived in shelters made of corn stalks stuck into the ground, covered with more stalks or with brown tents.

When they reached the boat, she found it was a fairly rude piece of workmanship, some distance from the water. However, the women and children were loaded into it, and a sheep, a kid, a supply of corn bread, cooking vessels and bedclothes were rather indiscriminately tumbled in among them. The men pushed the boat, almost upsetting it a time or two before they reached marshy water. Eventually the water was deep enough so they were able to get in and begin rowing. The people aboard came to about forty persons in all. It was after sunset when they reached the edge of a small bay and started to build a fire in the sand.

Miss Thompson had supposed they would be back home by nightfall and was concerned because she knew Mrs. Harvey would be expecting them. But the company was in no hurry. They killed the animals and put them to roast in the open fire, along with fresh fish. The latter were very good, though unsalted, eaten with some of the corn bread. One of the men described the bread as having been made half of chopped straw and sand and half of cornmeal!

A small group of the men who had gone off earlier in search of a ruined temple were several hours late in getting back, and their wives were very anxious about them. With the aid of signal fires and much loud shouting they were finally brought back to camp, but everyone was tired and hungry and a terrible quarrel broke out. Anna was very alarmed, though others tried to tell her it was really not of much importance. Eventually one of the men kissed his opponent's hand and peace was restored. The meat was cooked finally and passed around. One of the men brought Anna a piece in his hand, with some of the corn bread, which had been kept warm in the lap of one of the women. Anna said she was too hungry to ask any questions. She just tried to remember that she was camping in the desert.

When the women decided it was time to "retire," Anna suggested to one of the Christian men that they should have prayers. He asked where she thought she was! So she gathered up a group of the women, asked the people near the fire to be quiet for a moment, and herself led in prayer. The women then lay down on a piece of tent, Miss Thompson first making a pillow for herself out of piled-up sand, much to the amusement of the others. She lay long awake, listening to the men by the fire and the night birds, and thinking of the time when the Thompson family had camped by the Missouri River after the steamboat accident that brought about her mother's death. She thought that her mother would be uneasy about her if she knew she was sleeping on the ground in the desert. But she was also annoyed by the sand fleas and by her inability to stretch out her long legs without getting them into someone's face.

When a bright moon came up and shone in her eyes, she knew sleep was out of the question. So she took one of the wakeful children with her to the fire and softly sang some Arabic psalms, to the youngster's delight. Before sunrise all were up and sharing a breakfast of fish, eaten from branches of bushes instead of plates. Then they started off on a very long, tiresome walk across the sand to the temple ruins. It was a desolate place, but the ruins were unusual with a great deal of iridescent glass and pottery fragments scattered about. After retracing the weary walk, they embarked on their journey home and the men rowed hard for over three hours. The women had to be carried through the marshy landing place to a dry spot where they could sit and wait for the horses and donkeys. Everyone was hungry, so more fish were roasted and eaten with corn bread given them by nearby villagers. A boy brought pea stalks from a field close by and they ate these with great relish. Anna finally reached home at dusk, almost too tired to get up the stairs.

As the hot weather drew near, Anna arranged with another of the single women in the mission to go to Syria for a holiday, stopping in Alexandria for a few days on the way. This visit happened to include the Fourth of July, and the Americans at the mission were invited to a party given by a Greek who had spent some years in the States. Anna reported that it was a sorrowful evening for her as it turned out to be a regular dance. "The middle of the night was drawing near, and the gay music, fancy dresses, loaded table, etc. had no attraction for me and I never was so much turned against dancing," she wrote in her diary.

The party traveled to Beirut on a Russian steamer and went on to their rented house in Bahamdun on Mt. Lebanon, "six hours by (slow) horse." They had happy visits with other vacationing missionaries in Zahle and Bludan, enjoying the fruit and the scenery, but almost going over backwards on their donkeys on some of the steep trails. Dr. Johnston escorted the ladies on a strenuous horseback ride to see the ruins of Baalbec, but they were advised not to visit Damascus because of the prevalence of sickness at the time. As they started home, they had an opportunity to meet Dr. Cornelius Van Dyck, the biblical scholar and Arabic expert, in Beirut.

The return to Sinnoris was almost blocked by the unusual height of the September flood of the Nile. They were cut off from the world for more than a week, and their baggage, which had been left at Wasta, was delayed more than three weeks. Before long the Harveys were compelled to return to Cairo, partly for health reasons, and for some months the young headmistress was "chief manager of affairs." For part of the time she had only a blind girl to help her in the Sinnoris school. Many of the girls were very poor and could scarcely be spared from their duties at home. (These parents, as usual, put little value on the education of daughters. If the girls needed clothing for school they had somehow to make their dresses themselves.) In addition to the running of the schools, Miss Thompson was by this time supervising the teaching of about sixty women in their homes.

Meantime Dr. Harvey was struggling with a translation of the Psalms into a metrical version. He wrote to Anna just before Christmas to say how distressed he was to leave her alone so long.

The translation had finally reached Psalm 147. He said that Dr. Lansing, a poet from Latakia, and he had sent the first proof sheets back to the printer in Alexandria, adding, "It will be a valuable and much needed work when completed."

Miss Thompson took a two-week holiday in Cairo through New Year's and returned with Mrs. Harvey and the three small daughters. Little Annie, a great favorite and the namesake of "Auntie Thompson," fell ill in May and died of scarlet fever in a few days' time. The new church had just been dedicated and the first service to be held in it was the child's funeral, conducted by her grief-stricken father. The tiny body was laid by the north wall of the new church. Visitors to the grave some fifty years later stepped into the church and were interested to see the old iron frames of the pews which had been sent from the United States. These visitors were reminded of the benches in the one-room schools of long ago.

The young missionary's work in Sinnoris was terminated when the Harveys left for America on furlough, and she was transferred to the girls' school in Cairo. She was able, however, to make a few visits back to the Fayoum in the succeeding months. One memorable trip was to participate in the installation of the first Egyptian pastor in Sinnoris, the Rev. Shenooda Hanna.

A boarding school for girls had been opened in 1874 in a rented house in the Faggala (Radish Market) section of Cairo with Miss Eliza Johnston and Miss Margaret Smith in charge. They labored under the greatest difficulties, as the parents interfered continually, often trying to stay overnight in the school. They wanted to see what the girls were being given to eat and how they slept. The mothers came so frequently and were so untidy and noisy that they seriously interfered with the efficiency of the school. It took several months to convince them that their daughters were being well cared for and could be left to the attention of the superintendents and teachers. At the end of 1876 the day school and the boarding school were combined, and Miss Smith asked to be relieved so that she could give her attention to the work in Haret es Sakkain.

This section of Cairo was Miss Smith's great love until the end of her long career. In the spring of 1869 the Haret es Sakkain school, with all its friends and patrons, had been specifically cursed by the Coptic patriarch. Because of this anathema all but fifteen of the girls stopped attending, but as time passed they gradually drifted back. No missionary had been available to make visits in the homes and by

1875 the annual report said the women's prayer meeting was attended by from two to three! Not a very hospitable atmosphere, but Miss Smith was not daunted. Later there were four daughters of Arabi Pacha in attendance at this school, as well as several other girls from prominent Muslim families. When the oldest daughter of Arabi Pacha was to be married (in 1890), the missionaries, including Miss Thompson, were honored guests. An English lady visitor joined the group and she "had an instrument for taking photographs," so pictures went to the father in exile in Ceylon. The bride had not been allowed to stay long in the school, but she had a Bible in which she read every day. However, her new husband soon put a stop to that.

The Haret es Sakkain school was in a picturesque part of the old city. In some places the street was so narrow that the latticed bay windows of the second floors came very close together. Sometimes the missionaries held a meeting for the women where groups in two houses on opposite sides of the street were involved.

At the boarding school in Faggala Miss Thompson and Miss Johnston worked hard to make the girls have a happy life as well as keep up with their studies. New Year's Eve was usually a lively time, with a party and a decorated tree. (Christmas was celebrated otherwise, if at all.) The presents were certainly simple by today's standards—crochet hooks, needle books, handkerchiefs, and the like—but they were appreciated by the pupils. The singing, in Arabic and English, was always a successful part of the program.

The daily routine was enlivened by visits not only from the mission staffs of other stations but also by the arrival of famous personalities from abroad. Miss Thompson carried a large share of the housekeeping responsibilities and entertaining. Overseeing the cleaning and baking apple pies were part of her routine. Sabbaths were spent very seriously. There was morning service in Arabic, a Bible lesson with the girls in the afternoon, recitation of the catechism after tea, and then Miss Johnston read to them from the new Arabic church history!

During the late winter a new school for girls was opened in the district by the Coptic Orthodox Church, and the American school began to lose pupils. The patriarch had given a special blessing to those who attended his new school and the priests were working hard to gather in the girls. Miss Anna Y thought this was natural, though she found it hard to lose the pupils she had come to know

and love. Some people told her not to be concerned, that the new
school would not last long because the parents would not continue
to pay the required tuition. She discovered one element in the
situation that made her really happy. Nearly all the teachers had
been recruited from former staff members or students of the mission
school and they were continuing the Bible teaching they had been
accustomed to in their former school.

There was always something interesting to see in the streets. One
day they watched the strange spectacle then celebrated on Muhammed's birthday. Between a double line of friends and relatives, about
three hundred men marched in a line to the accompaniment of
drums, chanting the Koran in a kind of frenzy. They lay down on
their faces in the muddy road, close together, and a man on
horseback rode over their prostrate bodies. Some of the men were
able to get up and walk away but others were carried off
unconscious or in pain.

By the following December the mission building in Ezbekieh was
sufficiently completed for Miss Thompson, Miss Johnston, and Miss
Smith to move in, bringing the boarding girls. This was the beginning
of a school that soon became the best known in the country and the
greatest source for teachers for many decades. When the full school
opened on December 19, the girls were given a slip of paper to say
that from then on they would be expected to bring five piasters a
month for tuition—about twenty-five cents in those days. There was
great consternation and the pupils scattered "like a flock of sheep"
to the English and Coptic schools. Even those who brought the
money the first month were scarcely to be persuaded that they were
expected to do so each month. Some were kept on as charity pupils
through the generosity of a local gambler. Some were supported by
gifts from missionary societies in the States and frequently deficits
were made up out of Miss Anna Y's pocket. Word reached the school
that expenses must still be cut and this meant dismissing two of the
teachers. Christmas vacation became a time of weeping when the
teachers learned of this. Miss Thompson wrote home that "it was
pretty hard for me to tell the girls that I had formerly urged to come
to our school to go to other schools when they told me they had no
money for their tuition."

While the school was on vacation, Miss Thompson and Miss Smith
went to Fayoum to carry out a heavy program of home visiting. The
donkey provided for Anna for the journey to Sinnoris was so small

that she could cross her feet under it as she rode. The effect was so ludicrous that they dismounted and walked out of town before getting on again. Unhappily one of their reasons for going was to make arrangements to close the school at this station—another effect of the shortness of funds.

At Ezbekieh the enrollment gradually picked up again. Miss Thompson made a great many visits in homes and reported that "a new face brought new pupils." There were some discomforts in the new building—smoking heaters for the bath water, carpenters banging away all day, etc. But this was the beginning of fifteen years of devoted service by Miss Anna Y in that particular school. Three years later the building work was still going on and a letter home reported that a girl carrying mortar had fallen from the scaffolding and been badly hurt.

Miss Smith and Miss Thompson were sharing the same language teacher, a young man on the school staff named Ahmed Fahmy. When Anna had completed the Arabic Grammar with Ahmed she was told by the mission association that she didn't need a teacher any longer, since she could now pronounce the "ain" so well. In order to save expense, she stopped her formal lessons.

As Ahmed read the New Testament with Miss Smith, he decided he wanted to become a Christian, and this was the start of one of the most exciting stories in the mission's history. He came of a good family, and they were very devout Muslims. In a long letter, of which a copy still exists, Ahmed told Miss Smith that he was a Christian, but asked her not to mention it to his family until he could leave the country. Miss Smith and Miss Anna Y were concerned, but happy too, as both had been praying earnestly for him. The men in the mission thought Ahmed would be safer if he would come to the mission building where he would be under foreign protection, and this he did. Various members of his family came and pleaded with him to return, bringing famous Muslim scholars to argue with him. Then his brother, who had been a teacher in the mission school for ten years, accused Ahmed of receiving a bribe of a hundred pounds, of wanting an American wife, and of planning to go to the United States. He also accused him of stealing some books, listing ones he had given to Ahmed. Their father went to the sheikh of the Azhar and to the viceroy to lodge complaints against the mission. The former is said to have replied that Ahmed should be burned to death; the latter that the father could do nothing since freedom of religion was guaranteed.

Miss Thompson describes in her diary the affecting scene on November 25, 1877, when Dr. Lansing baptized Ahmed and received him into the church. Many of the audience wept but some were unhappy that he had not taken a new Christian name.

A few days later three men came to the mission in a closed carriage and succeeded in kidnapping Ahmed. Information was given to the British consul general and he promised to do all he could in the matter. Local gossip made the missionaries fear that the government had sent him up the Nile into exile. Miss Smith was unable to sleep all that night, and in the morning she got up, determined to go to see Ahmed's mother. She hoped to find out what had happened and to appeal to his parents. When the servants learned her plans, they tried very hard to dissuade her, but she got on her donkey and rode off alone into the Muslim section of town where Ahmed's family lived. A servant girl opened the door a few inches and Miss Smith pushed in, but the girl said, "Don't come in. A man was killed here last night." She said the women of the family had gone away, but Miss Smith was quite sure they were there. Although she was finally forced to leave, she noticed several things that convinced her that Ahmed was in the house. This was later confirmed and British and German officials busily intervened. There was great excitement in the city. The opinions among most Muslims were that the whole affair was due to Ahmed's wanting to marry a Christian; therefore the solution would be for the family to marry him quickly to a Muslim girl and get everything settled. The viceroy urged patience, as he did not believe that harm would come to Ahmed in his own father's house.

Word came from the vice-consul that a man called Ahmed had reported he was recanting from his Christian baptism after reading more books. But during dinner on New Year's Day they had more convincing proof. Ahmed arrived at the mission with members of his family, asking for his clothes and books and saying that he had gone back to Islam. (He told someone privately that he had gone through enough torture "to turn the head of a child gray.") This was a terrible blow to Miss Anna Y and Miss Smith, but the next day Ahmed slipped back again like a thief, his head wrapped in a shawl, to tell them he had been forced to say what he did. They had made him sleep between his father and his brother or he would have escaped through a window earlier.

It was legal then under Islamic law to kill an apostate if he could not be persuaded to return to the faith within three days. When the Muslim teachers brought by his father were not able to convince Ahmed, the family had secured a key to an empty house and arranged for him to be taken there, where some hired Greeks were to kill him. On the occasions when he had been summoned to the consulate his brother had kept a gun on him. His father had paid a man to write a potent charm that could prevent him from leaving Islam and had it sewed into his *tarboush.* (When he tore it out later, Miss Thompson told him he should have left it there to prove it had no power.) A few days after circumstances caused the failure of the plot with the Greek killers, Ahmed's mother discovered he was to be poisoned. She warned him not to accept food or even a cigarette from his father or his brother.

Having finally made his way safely to the mission, Ahmed stayed closely indoors. He did some translation work and gave Miss Thompson help with her classes. She was a member of the group that held several long consultations about Ahmed's future and the advisability of his leaving the country. He held fast through many trying weeks. In March Lord and Lady Aberdeen took him secretly to Scotland. There they assisted in his further education, leading to his later career as a medical missionary in China. In 1880, when Miss Thompson stopped in Scotland on her way home for furlough, she was able to visit Ahmed. Nearly twenty years later, as the good doctor and his family went through Suez, his old friend and pupil, Miss Smith, was able to go down to the boat and see him once more.

Lord and Lady Aberdeen also rescued some little slave boys in Upper Egypt, paying seven pounds each for them. They gave them Scottish names and put them in school in Assiut. One afternoon these boys overheard some little slave girls talking in the street, using their own African language. Apparently they were survivors of the dreaded forty-day trek and had been brought into Assiut for sale. The boys ran back to the school and told the missionaries, but they were unable to do much unless the girls could be got onto mission property. So the boys gathered up some friends and staged their own slave raid, carrying the girls off to the American College where they could be protected.

Lord Cromer sent twelve freed slave girls to the Ezbekieh school to be under Miss Thompson's care. Their health was very precarious as the change in the climate from the Sudan brought on tuberculosis in a number of cases. All but one of these twelve became Christians and some were very devoted workers in the hospital and the schools. Miss Anna Y agreed to take the girls, partly in the hope that they might some day become teachers among their own people. They had no knowledge of their parents or their family religion, but their former owners had given them Muslim names. Some of the girls were a little refractory at first, thinking that the missionary would baptize them. They kept their adopted names, except for two who had the same name. One of these was renamed Susan, this being the nearest approach to Assuan! She was from Nubia and remembered being carried away by the *mahdi* and later playing with his children. One day, when the youngsters were getting gum from a tree, a man on horseback snatched her up and carried her off. She was an attractive nine-year-old, singing and dancing and keeping happy in spite of her memories of being passed from one person to another.

The school cook, herself a freed slave from the Sudan, took a great interest in these girls, and during the summer vacation she started a prayer meeting with those who were willing to attend. Little Susan was one of the first to learn to pray her own prayers, and she began to work hard to earn a little money for the missionary society. She was doing well in her schoolwork too, and was devoted to Miss Thompson. When it came time for Miss Anna Y's furlough, Susan sobbed, "I shall never see her again, I shall never see her again!" After the summer vacation she seemed to fail gradually in health, and by April she was in the hospital with consumption. As long as she could talk without too much pain and coughing, she read from her beloved Bible to the other patients. She had asked to be baptized before Miss Thompson left for home, but as she was so young and still in school, the staff thought it should be delayed for a while. Now she began to ask for baptism again and insisted that it should be done in church. Since that was impossible, the sacrament was finally administered in the hospital. When someone asked her if she was afraid to die, she answered with a strong, "*No.*" She passed away the next night. The girls missed her in their Sabbath evening meetings, as she had memorized several Epistles and most of John's Gospel and would quote from her favorite passages, though at the last her voice could scarcely be heard.

Three more of these girls died, but the others made good records as household helpers, practical nurses, and teachers' helpers. One became a Bible woman in Cairo under Miss Thompson's direction. Another became matron of the girls' boarding school, then under the superintendency of Miss Ella Kyle. This former slave was a consecrated Christian and so competent that she was able to relieve the missionary of considerable responsibility. Miss Kyle admitted to being selfishly afraid that someone would want her as his wife, and she dreaded losing her. One of the girls was married from the school as it was the only home she had ever known.

The headmistress was distressed to observe some snobbery among the other students after the slave girls were admitted. There had been no apparent class consciousness before this, and she felt this new element in the school family had proved rather disturbing to some of the pupils. When one of the missionaries asked a Cairo girl why she did not attend Miss Thompson's school, the answer was that "girls with bare feet go there!"

As a contrast, the school had one alumna who was a *maharani*. The romantic tale began before Miss Thompson came to the school, but she knew the family and saw much of them on their visits to Cairo. Her diary mentions several times that she had gone to Shepheard's Hotel to see the princess Bamba. This was the story. In 1839 the maharajah of the Punjab died, and eleven of his wives were burned on his funeral pyre. He was the famous warrior Ranjeet Singh, owner of the Kohinoor diamond which is now among the British crown jewels. His estate was inherited by his four-year-old son, Dhuleep Singh, who later became a Christian. The British took over the kingdom after a fight with the Sikhs, and Dhuleep Singh was taken to England where he was given a large estate and a very handsome annuity. He visited Egypt on a trip to India by special permission of the British government to take his mother's body home. While in Egypt he took the opportunity to see some of the work of the mission. At the school he saw one of the pupils named Bamba. She was the daughter of an Ethiopian slave woman and a German merchant, a very sweet and attractive girl and a true Christian. The prince told the missionaries that he did not want to marry an English wife, but his wife must be a Christian, and he said he would like to marry Bamba. He realized she was young and unsophisticated, but he trusted the American wives would help her receive the training she would need. Then he went on to Bombay. This astounding proposal raised questions in everybody's mind, not least of all Bamba's. She wanted to stay and eventually teach in her school, but after much prayer it was finally decided to send her acceptance to the maharajah. The wedding was a quiet one, the bride not at all aware of the value of the jewels she was wearing. But she was happy the next week to present a gift of $5,000 to the mission. The gift was repeated annually for fifteen years, a thank offering from Dhuleep Singh for his bride. The houseboat, the *Ibis,* on which they took a belated honeymoon on the Nile, was presented later to the mission as well, and it was done many years of faithful service up and down the river.

Their position in England was next that of the royal family, and Queen Victoria stood as godmother to some of their six children. They lived on a magnificent estate in Elvedon and all went well until the maharajah became entangled with some unsavory companions. After getting him into debt, they persuaded him that he had been cheated by the British government: He finally went to Russia, renouncing his Christian faith because it was the religion of the nation that had defrauded him, as he had come to believe. This was a heavy blow to his wife and family, and Bamba did not live long afterwards. It happened that Dr. and Mrs. Lansing had been called to England at that time and were able to go to her. The princess died in the arms of her spiritual mother after a wonderful life of devotion and faith, Ezbekieh School's most famous alumna.

Miss Thompson received some encouragement over her efforts with the school from Dr. Lansing, who visited the school practically every day. He said that her girls had learned to think and to study and displayed better habits of thought than he saw in some of the boys' schools. He did not know whether the girls were smarter or whether it was due to the teaching methods they were using in the school. One element that contributed to the success of the school was surely the personal attention each girl received. Miss Anna Y, in all the schools where she worked, soon learned to know the pupils individually, and there was always a word or a smile for each of them. This was something all children noticed about Miss Thompson—they were never ignored, talked down to, or given divided attention. Those who speak of her today remember how surprised they were, and even flattered, as youngsters when she took so much time to show her real interest in them.

Sometimes it took a great deal of patience to control the mischief and real naughtiness among the schoolgirls. The teachers had their ways of making trouble too. One day, when a certain teacher was put in charge temporarily, another became so enraged that she went into convulsions. There was always outside criticism to be borne. Once when Miss Anna Y called at the home of a pupil, the mother flew at her "like a hornet" because the girl had not learned to sew well. Occasionally bulletins would go out from Muslim authorities, warning people not to be taken in by the foreign Christian schools—under the guise of teaching girls book learning and handcrafts they actually were "sowing seeds of blasphemy in their hearts," they said.

Sometimes the school was swamped with crowds of tourists arriving on cruises, but more often there were individuals to be guided about and shown the work. In January, 1878, the school was honored by a visit from General and Mrs. Ulysses S. Grant. Mrs. Grant with a friend, Mrs. General Stone, came up into the house and met the girls. They were interested in their handwork and Mrs. Grant asked for a motto one of the pupils had made—"I am the Light of the world." She was vexed because they had been delayed at an earlier appointment and had not reached the school before dismissal. Miss Anna Y was invited to a party for General and Mrs. Grant and later called on them at the Palace Hotel. On Sabbath evening the distinguished visitors attended the English service at the mission, driving up in style with postillions. Miss Thompson described Mrs. Grant's costume of purple velvet and gray fur and remarked that she seemed not to be used to sitting on such hard seats, judging from the way she twisted around!

Miss Thompson's sparkling enthusiasm was a little dimmed through the late spring of 1878, partly over concern for the young convert, Ahmed, and also over the prospect of losing her colleague, Miss Johnston. She was planning to go home to be away more than a year, and the separation made Miss Anna Y very desolate. She felt quite inadequate to carry the full responsibility of the school, and time after time her diary reads, "Feeling blue today." Then she wrote, "I have been a great deal exercised over my rebellious feelings these times, especially in view of Miss Johnston's going away. I was much impressed with the text, 'Have faith in God' but it seems as if I do not want to trust Him." Several times she admitted to feeling tired out, but as she had previously recorded visiting seven homes in an afternoon, that would not seem very surprising.

After busy preparations the teachers held an examination for the boarding school in mid-March with a large crowd of visitors, including travelers from overseas. Dr. Watson examined the girls in Bible History and distributed the prizes. Others examined them in Arabic Grammar, and the showing that the girls made pleased the crowd a great deal. Egyptians love their language, just the sound of it, if it is well pronounced and rhythmical, whether or not they can catch the meaning. Arabic Grammar is sufficiently difficult for anyone, so that a schoolgirl's grasp of it impressed the audience. The handwriting and sewing exhibits and the girls' singing were well received too. Miss Thompson reported that several of those present congratulated the staff and "called down blessings."

The senior class examinations were held a few days later when the missionaries were in the city for their association meeting. Dr. Hogg examined the boys in Moral Philosophy (!) and one of the Egyptian teachers was in charge of the Astronomy test. The girls were examined in Geography, Arabic Grammar, and Arithmetic. Later the whole group sang with Dr. Harvey "pointing on the modulator." Each of the graduates delivered an oration, some of them full of "poetical jingle," as Miss Anna Y put it. The lad who took first prize in English delivered a speech on "The Advantages of Travel." Diplomas had been prepared on heavy paper, beautifully written by a country boy in the junior class, and then tied with red tape in the absence of ribbon. One of the men teachers "delivered or read a high flown something," a number of prizes were handed out, and Dr. Lansing closed what must have been an exhausting evening with a few remarks of his own.

After struggling for some time with a cold and finally losing her voice, Miss Thompson took to her bed. Then she remembered Zechariah and wondered whether she had lost her voice for want of faith that God would take care of them after Miss Johnston left. When word came that she had been officially appointed to fill Miss Johnston's place during her absence, Miss Anna Y wrote, "This going away of Miss Johnston has been like a nightmare to me for six months, and now she is really gone, and Dr. Watson as well, the two persons on whom we have always relied both for management and advice. May God give us wisdom. But it was sad to part with them." Miss Smith stepped into the breach, taking over the sewing and two of Anna's former classes so that she could cover Miss Johnston's work. Dr. Harvey assumed Dr. Watson's former duty of conducting opening exercises for the girls and teaching the English class. The masons had reached the point of laying the steps in the building, accompanied by constant thumping and clouds of dust. For the next few weeks they were plagued with illness, generally with two or three of the staff or the boarders sick in bed at once. Sore throats, physics, gargles and special diets were the order of the day. Sometimes it was hard for Anna to fit everything in that she was expected to do. She had been going to the boys' school twice a week to teach them singing, but she was not able to keep that up, although they were doing well and she had become fond of the lads. When school finally closed, it took her ten days to store the furniture and equipment so that whitewashing and painting could be done. Some of the girls had no homes to go to, so Mrs. Harvey took some of them and Miss Thompson took one with her to the summer mission house in Ramleh on the seashore. There was no thought of being idle, however; the little girl was given English lessons and Miss Smith taught the Muslim gardener to read (from the Bible) while Anna undertook to teach the cook, also a Muslim.

On their return to Cairo there was a month's confusion while the painting was completed. One of the new apartments was finally finished and the Lansings moved in above the school. As Miss Thompson came in from making calls one evening, she met two men asking for the American school. One said he was an American and followed her upstairs. He said he had been born in Suez but had gone to the States with his German father. (His mother had been Muslim, from Egypt.) After working for several years in a circus, he had heard Dr. Dwight L. Moody preach a sermon on the thief on the cross and he had been converted. Local clergymen befriended the former lion tamer but he ran away when he was sent to school. He worked his way to England, Japan, India, and finally Egypt. His story was that he wanted to be a missionary, but he turned out to be a remarkable liar. One evening he threw his Testament into the fireplace in Dr. Harvey's living room, saying he would shave his head to show the world he had died a Muslim, and then drown himself. Later "Arab Willie," as he was called, wept and confessed he was a sinner.

Certainly life was never dull at the school, and the headmistress needed to be full of ingenuity! But through all the vicissitudes Anna usually kept her composure, and the girls made good progress.

CHAPTER III

FIRSTFRUITS

One of the early pupils in the school when it opened in Faggala had been a girl named Miriam Ibrahim. She was a fine influence, taking time to read to the little girls and being generally helpful. Miss Johnston decided she had the makings of a good teacher and invited her to join the staff. A little later she was asked to make the sacrifice of giving her time and talent to the more difficult task of house visiting. Very few educated girls were willing to undertake this, being ashamed, as they said, to "go about knocking at people's doors." But Miriam conquered that hesitation and became an excellent worker who made friends easily by a very winning manner.

After two years of this work Miriam took ill. Her ignorant mother, who had no idea of how to care for her, refused for forty days to allow anyone even to see her. Miss Smith finally managed to get in and bathed the sick girl, who had not had even her face washed in all that time. The missionaries succeeded later in moving her into the Haret es Sakkain school building where they could care for her. But she gradually grew worse. When death seemed near, she asked Miss Thompson and Miss Smith to come and bring the teachers with them. She talked with them for a little while, sending a message to Miss Johnston in the States that she would not see her again in Cairo but hoped to meet her in heaven. Soon afterwards she was released from her pain and weakness.

When Miss Johnston got the word of her death, she wrote, "The first fruits of the boarding school! We had some dark days in the beginning of this work, and we often felt the burden pressing heavily; but I am sure that we feel well repaid when we look at the life and death of the lovely girl who has now been called home to be 'forever with the Lord.' I believe I express the feelings of my associates in the work when I say we should be grateful that we had the privilege of being her teachers, and it is worth all we have borne of trial and discouragement to see what God can do for us and through us." Miss Thompson, too, said that Miriam's death had made her even more concerned about keeping the little prayer groups going when attendance was small and she felt tempted to give them up.

The current session of the school certainly had its share of trials. The Catholic pupils led a kind of insurrection for a time. One of the other boarders did not seem able to adjust to school and began running away to relatives in a distant part of the city. After they had brought her back three times, and spanking did no good, Miss Anna Y tried the plan of tying her to another girl! Even that failed, and Anna said sadly, "Our school seems to be destined to become a prison." After the fifth escapade, word was sent to the girl's father that they could not keep her any longer. He sent a sister in her place who was very much happier, though "an odd genius," as Miss Anna Y put it. (Probably she meant to use the old expression, "an odd genus.")

Another girl from a Christian family decided that they had too many prayers in the school. Miss Thompson reminded her that she had known about the prayers before she came, and told her that if she didn't like them she need not stay. This brought on a flood of tears, as she interpreted the remark to mean that she must leave because she was a disgrace to the school. Later she wrote a little note to Miss Thompson (in French), asking her forgiveness, and they became good friends. The girls seemed to be in a half-unruly, half-thoughtless mood. "Wisdom needed," Miss Anna Y commented.

Occasionally the routine was enlivened by a wedding of one of their previous students. Miss Thompson described one such affair in some detail. Dinner at noon consisted of fourteen or fifteen courses. Later "confusion seemed to reign, especially with the seesaw music on the piano." She helped to dress the bride by the light of a single candle in someone's hand. The outfit was elaborate—white flowered silk trimmed with orange flowers, white satin slippers, kid gloves, tulle veil. The bride's jewelry, which was doubtless her dowry, included a watch, gold chain, diamond earrings, gold bracelets, rings, and locket. The ceremony was delayed, to show that the parents prized their daughter and did not want to lose her. A school friend who was to be married in the same ceremony, arrived about ten in the evening. The wedding procession had been stopped frequently along the way by people bringing out sweet drinks to the crowd. When the second bride finally reached the door, the house slaves refused permission for her to enter until they were given a present. This was customary, but the American visitors were alarmed, fearing that the brides' dresses would be ruined and the brides themselves would be trampled to death in the crush.

Miss Thompson and one of the other mission women led the two brides to the front of the crowded parlor and seated them beside their bridegrooms. The ceremony included a long sermon and many prayers and lasted an hour and a half, so it was midnight when they were seated for another large dinner. Two days later Miss Anna Y and a friend called on the brides. One bridegroom was vexed with his new wife because she was not dressed as he thought proper. Miss Anna Y agreed with him, and the girl finally burst into tears. Not a very satisfactory visit, Anna said.

Miss Johnston returned to the school in the autumn of 1879. At the close of the first term the two headmistresses went together to Fayoum. Their ride to Sinnoris took place after dark, and the donkey men were so afraid of robbers that they would not allow the women to speak. They made a great many calls in Sinnoris homes and found a case of measles in nearly every one. When they had returned to Cairo, Anna came down with what she thought was a heavy cold, but it turned out to be measles, so that she was in bed for a fortnight. The girls were not allowed in that part of the house and Miss Johnston cared for her, keeping the school open. Everyone was relieved that it was not smallpox, which had been feared at first.

When Anna recovered, she wrote to Dr. Dales to tell him that she was asking the mission association to allow her to go home. She had had no furlough in the eight years since leaving home. The association approved her going and the next weeks were busy ones, filled with packing and interruptions along with the usual school duties. The girls brought her little gifts they had made, and a large crowd turned up at the station to see her off. She had been feeling so discouraged earlier that she thought if ever she got home she

would certainly stay there, but she found it hard to say goodbye
when the time came.

The furlough was a happy one and passed quickly. When Anna
returned for her second term, she found that the school enrollment
was growing and the financial situation had eased somewhat. There
are frequent comments in the annual reports and in letters to friends
about generous help provided by visitors. Sometimes it was a pound
or two, which usually went to support a special girl in school. Often
it was a gift of time and talent. For some time the wife of a British
general came regularly to teach the girls drawing and Bible, in
French. Three friends from Edinburgh were so impressed by these
Presbyterian mission workers, and by what they had done for British
soldiers in Cairo, that they started a fund among Scottish churches.
Several hundred pounds were sent to Cairo and used to build a new
school, also used as a church, in the Bulak section of the city. Miss
Thompson took the greatest interest in both the school and the
church, and gave a great deal of help to both.

Miss Johnston was married in 1881 and went with her missionary
husband to India; and once again the full responsibility of the
boarding school fell on Miss Anna Y. Three years later she was able
to report an attendance of a hundred and seventy girls, the
thirty-four boarders using the full facilities of that department. She
was happy to say that twenty-six of the girls who had been boarders
in the school had made public confession of their Christian faith.

During this period frequently the only entry in her diary is
"Busy." She was besieged by requests to find teachers for other
schools from among her graduates, but it was difficult to secure the
parents' agreement. Undoubtedly it was dangerous for a young woman
to go into a town where there was no mission family or pastor's
home where she could be looked after. It was unheard of for a single
girl to live alone. (Even as late as the 1940's Egypt's first aviatrix
created a stir in Cairo by deciding to leave her parents' home and
take her own apartment.) However, where suitable living arrangements could be made, many of Miss Thompson's young graduates
became splendid teachers. The Ezbekieh school had to reduce
expenses and let some of its alumnae teachers go. They were quickly
snapped up by other schools. After visiting the boarding school, one
English visitor wrote, "Sitting side by side were Mohammedans,
Copts, Syrians, Jews, Sudanese and others, the girls displaying
picturesque costumes which would greatly amuse our English

children. As I addressed about a hundred and twenty of the girls and was interpreted, I thought they displayed as great a share of quickness and intelligence as English children do." He might have been even less patronizing if he had been able to talk with these students in their own language.

In a letter to the missionary society of the First Ohio presbytery in May, 1887, Anna reported on the girls' progress, especially seven whom she had known as babies in her days in Fayoum. She wrote, "My mission life will soon count sixteen years. I find that as I grow older many things do not worry me as much as they did long ago. I have learned at least that the earth is the Lord's and the work here is His work, but it seems to me that I worry more now perhaps than formerly about the health of the girls, and over the funds of the school. I worry especially about the Sudanese girls who do not bear the climate well and often decline rapidly with consumption. I find it very hard sometimes to satisfy the appetites of the girls without grudging the outlay, especially since word came from the Board that mission expenses must be cut at least $3,000 this year." She described her difficulties in trying to get along with one teacher less than before, then added, "I went so far as to say that if it were not that two societies at home were supporting me, I would volunteer to go home 'on the reduction of the strength.' "

The school year 1889-90 had its special trials. The Coptic holidays disrupted the first month and then an epidemic of influenza struck the staff and pupils. Sometimes eight at a time were ill in bed in the school, and it went on for a full month. Not a teacher escaped, and often a third of the students were absent. Miss Thompson had another difficulty not experienced by heads of schools in America—no one language could be used with the entire school or staff. Most understood Arabic but several had to be spoken to in French, Italian, or English. It was hard to supervise a teacher who knew neither Arabic nor English, when the headmistress knew little French.

After fifteen years in the school, in February of 1890, Miss Anna Y asked to be relieved and allowed to go home on furlough. She suggested that she spend the last two months of her term working in the villages so that a new headmistress could prepare the June examinations. The association approved this plan and she joined Dr. and Mrs. Chauncey Murch on the houseboat, helping with the evangelistic work and seeing old friends everywhere. She missed no opportunity to visit the schools along the way, especially those in Assiut.

Anna's leave-taking at the school was a sad time for everybody. She wrote later, "I thank God for the privilege I have had in the school of training teachers, wives and mothers. May God forgive my neglect of duty and accept any service for His glory, done in His name." The school arranged a great reception before she left, giving her a gold pencil, which she prized for many years, and money to buy Stanley's new book. About fifty people went to the railway station afterwards to see her off.

A copy survives of a paper Miss Thompson prepared for a Young People's Institute in Xenia, Ohio, during that visit home. In it she speaks glowingly of the Egyptian theological students, twenty-five in the class, who, in addition to their studies, were active in various meetings in the churches and slum homes. One whom she mentioned particularly was blind, but he could repeat whole chapters of the Bible and was one of the best in learning the church tunes. Characteristically she did not mention that she had taken time two or three days a week to teach their music class. She praised the progress the girls in the school were making, and the devotion of some of them in the missionary societies and *zenana* work. She added, "The government has been raising the standard of its schools and founding new ones in the large towns. . . . The Bible is not allowed in these government schools. In one school in Cairo the boys were much offended because the words 'in the year of Christ' occurred in their history lesson. . . . There is only one government school for girls. The Inspector is a Scotchman and the matron a Syrian Protestant, but the Christian religion must not be spoken of. . . . Our Mission has a hundred and four different places for the education of Egyptians, and there are forty-seven Sabbath schools. But now one will say, as of the loaves and fishes, what are these among so many?" She ended with a fervent appeal for more workers to help the young people of Egypt.

A few years later she could report thirteen mission schools for girls. In some of the village schools a few girls were also allowed to attend the boys' school, but that usually meant listening to whatever they could catch from behind a curtain! One interesting student at this time in the Cairo boarding school was an older girl, a Muslim, who was so religious that she had already made the pilgrimage to Mecca four times. She decided to become a doctor to help her

Egyptian sisters and was advised to enter the mission school. She began to attend the prayer meeting and before long she was taking part, always closing her prayers with the name of Christ. It would have been unthinkable to Miss Thompson that the day would come when the government would forbid the teaching of the Bible in her old school to all but girls from Christian families. Or that an American teacher would be deported because she had answered frankly when a Muslim pupil, willing to trap her, asked her pointed questions about her Christian faith.

When Miss Anna Y returned to Cairo in November, 1891, she was asked to take charge of some of the house visiting and supervision of several of the Bible women, but she continued as well to give help to the schools and never lost interest in their welfare. A colleague wrote home, "Miss Thompson has plunged into work again with all the might she has. I wonder how long she will be able to keep up, or hold out, at the rate she has begun." Her home with Mrs. Harvey was always open to the teachers and it was not unknown for them to entertain all of the girls' schoolteachers for dinner—forty of them! When Miss Anna Y saw that her meeting for women and girls on Wednesday afternoons in the Bulak school was interfering with the order of the school, she promptly moved out and held it in the nearby "huts," as they were appropriately called. The women had been finding it a good social occasion and were arriving more than an hour early, as well as staying after the meeting for their reading lessons with their respective teachers. A former headmistress could not allow this kind of disruption to continue, although leaving the school meant a great deal of inconvenience for her and her helpers.

Another little school Miss Thompson was supervising moved into a one-story building with a small yard. Miss Anna Y thought it was a very suitable location, until she discovered that men in the street found it entertaining to look in through the low windows. She didn't object when they seemed to be interested in listening to the Bible lesson, however. She was trying to get the children to pay something for tuition, and this kept some away. Children taking English lessons were asked for fifty cents a month, and for Arabic it was half a piaster (two and a half cents) or nothing.

In her annual report in 1900 Anna wrote that the increased demand for education for girls was bringing some difficulties, since the Copts were able to offer salaries to teachers that were two or three times what the American mission and the Evangelical church schools could pay. They lost some of their own alumnae as teachers for this reason. Since early marriage was the custom, it was hard to keep a teacher long enough to give her the necessary experience and maturity to fit her to be a head teacher. Sometimes young girls were made too much of by school committees and brought too prominently before the men of the town, with unhappy results, but most of them did well. There was still prejudice against them. Parents sometimes refused a girl as a prospective wife for their son if she had been a teacher, because they inferred she had done it out of poverty. A postal clerk who married one of the boarding school teachers was loud in his praises. He said, "I am pleased to say that I have found a good and virtuous wife. She is not at all like the others, who are only useful as drudges. I feel that I have gained a precious jewel."

The mission schools had a distinguished visitor in 1909—President Theodore Roosevelt. In a speech delivered during his time in Egypt he said, "I have known of your work for many years, and since I struck the station on the Sobat River I have been constantly a witness of the results of the work, and I have been particularly anxious to see the girls' schools, because I think that, more and more, everywhere it is growing to be realized that you cannot raise part of humanity while neglecting the other part, and that it is idle to try to raise the man unless the woman is raised at the same time." This is in some contrast to the Hindu proverb quoted in one of the early issues of the *Missionary Magazine:* "Educating a girl is like putting a knife in the hands of a monkey."

In the early 1900's new property was secured in the Faggala district and a girls' school was begun. Miss Thompson had oversight of this school from the time of her return from furlough in 1901, with Miss Laura Walker also helping. By 1904 they could report three hundred and thirty-seven pupils in the school. Many of the parents spoke appreciatively of what Miss Thompson and Miss Walker were doing to train their children for lives of usefulness. The school was in a good neighborhood and drew pupils from homes financially able to pay modest tuitions.

Another headmistress in Egypt, writing to the *Missionary Magazine,* spoke feelingly on this matter of tuitions. She said, "I wish I could make plain to you what a worry and vexation this collection of tuitions is. I am sure you would realize this, could you see how we have to stop, perhaps in the midst of hearing a recitation, to try to reason with someone who wants to put his girl in school, but who insists he is not able to pay the full amount asked. Perhaps after the class time is exhausted we succeed in getting him to pay, or on the contrary, see him go off saying he can't afford it, leaving us in doubt whether we did right or not by allowing the child, for the difference of a few piasters, to be cheated out of Christian training, and perhaps forever closing the door against her coming to a knowledge of the Saviour. Could you know all the ins and outs connected with school-keeping here, you would know we are trying to do our best to make the schools self-supporting, but with a great deal of worry and heaviness of heart; and then it must all be gone over again the next month, and the next, till the end of the school year. We are glad to welcome the holidays even if we have no snow or we fail to hear the jingle of bells."

About this time Miss Thompson described vividly the difficult first steps in opening still another little school. The people in the neighborhood had begged her to make a start, promising a large number of girls willing to pay twenty-five cents a month tuition, and arguing that the room would be available for meetings as well. So Miss Anna Y found a room and rented it, bought two seats, a rush mat, and a water jar, and they were ready. The room had good light, good enough during the opening prayers and Bible lesson for Anna to see that the many bugs in the walls were out on the warpath. The blind woman seated beside her was wearing a black robe, and one glance at it was enough to show that they had more than they had calculated on. So they took out the new furnishings, got the rent refunded, and located another room, which was to be cleaned and ready for them the following Monday. The story goes on: "When I went on Monday I found there was a big quarrel going on between our blind evangelist and the landlady because she had taken from us part of the rent to secure the bargain, and afterwards rented the rooms to a family of people who spent the night in it, but left the next day when they heard we had rented it, as they are friends of ours; and there was a quarrel because the landlady had given back only about a third of the rent for the month. It appeared afterward that some people had strongly advised her not to rent it for a school, as there might be night meetings when people could take advantage of an open house and steal."

Though much of Miss Thompson's time was now taken up with her supervision of the Bible women, at the 1920 meeting of the association she was asked to take as an additional assignment the care of the famous old school in Haret es Sakkain. Sometimes her day's schedule sounds a little fantastic—the morning in the Faggala school, then on to the little struggling one in Bulak; late in the afternoon a call at the British embassy.

By this time she was able to look back and begin to see some of the results of the earlier years' work. In 1919 she was invited with others of the mission to a reception for a Christian teacher who had made a name for herself after graduating from Cheltenham School in Britain. Miss Thompson had a happy time, for it was a gathering of teachers, children, and grandchildren of their work. The guest of honor had herself taught at the Ezbekieh school for three years.

After six years of uphill struggle in the little school in Bulak the missionaries were refused permission to continue renting the property and were forced to close the school. The one teacher had been handling forty-five pupils for some time. (But most of the other schools in Cairo were doing well. In 1925, Miss Roxy Martin, then head of the Ezbekieh school, held the graduation exercises at the Continental Hotel, not far from the mission. The American ambassador watched the graduates perform and announced that they would have done credit to Wellesley!) Once again friends in the States came to the rescue and the Bulak school was reopened. Sometimes Miss Thompson had to make up a small deficit personally, but later the Women's Board underwrote the budget as the rooms were used for the Sabbath school as well as the day school. It seemed rather a bargain—$90 per annum. But after thirteen years Miss Thompson reported that the evangelist's salary had been cut off, so they gave up the house "where the poor people were taught." Almost at once she was asked to help with still another school run by the church in Old Cairo, where a new school was running hard competition. So she added this to her weekly schedule. It is hard to assess Miss Thompson's contribution as a teacher and school administrator. She was not sparing of either her teachers or her pupils. A letter has been found that was evidently the draft of one she sent to a prospective staff member in 1887. She wrote, "We wish one who can teach Arabic grammar, arithmetic, physiology, and astronomy. It is necessary that our teacher should be good at cutting plain dresses, dressing gowns, underclothing, etc. and be able to teach the girls how to sew well, as well as a little fancy work. The food of the school is very plain as we have to be

very economical and for the same reason we cannot give a large
salary. You would of course have board and lodging in the school,
with washing; starched clothes you would have to manage yourself
with the help of the boarders. Lessons begin at half past eight and
close at half past four with an hour or an hour and a half at noon
according to the season, but it has been the custom of the head
teacher to have an extra hour at noon. Out of school hours it is
always the duty of the head teacher to look after the girls and their
work, with the help of another teacher, be able to take a Sabbath
school class, lead in prayer, etc. We have two months' vacation in
summer and ten days at Christmas and Easter. Health and patience
are necessary." She added "and so forth," but one wonders how
much more could be added without daunting the new applicant
completely.

However, anything Miss Thompson asked of her staff was even
more asked of herself. The priceless ingredient she added to the life
of the schools was her unlimited interest in every girl; a deep,
sensitive Christian love, always seasoned with a very sweet smile, a
song, and frequently a chuckle.

CHAPTER IV

BEARER OF THE GOOD NEWS

From the very first days of Miss Anna Y's life in Egypt she was an inveterate caller. These were more than social occasions, of course. They had a definite evangelistic purpose, and a Bible lesson was carefully chosen for each visit. Miss Thompson was intensely interested in people and she liked to see them in their homes. She also liked to have company on her calling expeditions. Of the hundreds of visitors to her home with Dr. and Mrs. Harvey in Cairo very few can have escaped her enthusiastic invitation, "Come, go with me. I'm going to Faggala," or Bulak or Old Cairo, or any of a dozen sections of town. One young lady, up to town for a few days' change from her intensive language study, accepted such an invitation and commented that it would be a new experience for her. Miss Thompson was shocked, not to say thunder-struck. "In the country ten months, and she's never been in an Arab home!" There's no doubt that Miss Anna Y would have made her own opportunities if they had not been so freely offered to her in her early days in Sinnoris.

Going calling with Miss Thompson opened the eyes of a great many new missionaries. The first lesson was that it was quite useless to set a schedule for visits and stick to it. One great problem is traditional Egyptian hospitality. A guest must always be offered food or drink, whether he wants it or not, and if he refuses it or tries to evade taking it, he may give mortal offense. In the poorer homes they are quick to ask, "Is our food not clean?" Sometimes the

coffee cups have been retrieved from among the shoes and other
articles under the bed, or the nuts have been politely cracked by the
hostess' teeth, but a missionary must learn to conquer any
squeamishness. Sometimes it was not easy for Miss Anna Y. One
evening, after a great many years in Egypt, she noted in her diary,
"The food too strong and hairy to be enjoyed." One of the mission
men on a village tour by houseboat, after enduring a meal of rough
bread and sour milk, said he wouldn't have decided to be a
missionary if he had known what he would have to eat!

But having got the refreshments out of the way, it took a while to
get down to the purpose of the call. She must ask about the
children—who may be making a good deal of noise at the time,
grabbing at the books or clothing of the visitors—and then *answer* a
great many questions if it is a first call, or if there is a new person in
the party. The first question will be whether she is married, and if
not, why not (with generous offers to help find a suitable husband);
the dress and petticoat material would probably be fingered and the
price of the cloth inquired about; sometimes surprise would be
expressed that anyone would leave home and parents to come to a
strange land, with a strong hint about the apparent absence of family
feeling. This last category of questions would finally open the way
for the visitor to explain why she was there with the good news of
the gospel. Miss Thompson made a point of reading a brief passage
from the Bible and getting one or more of the women in the room to
begin reading lessons from the same good textbook. Then, after
prayer, it was time to move on to another house and a new situation.

One morning, when Miss Anna Y had planned to hear the lessons
of several reading pupils in one neighborhood, she was completely
sidetracked. A Muslim woman who had been listening rushed up to
her and said, "Now you must come to my house and pray there."
Miss Thompson said she would try to go another day, but the
woman insisted that her house was near and she refused to be put
off. Racing ahead around one corner after another, she left Miss
Thompson bewildered and out of breath, while the men in the little
shops along the way made amused remarks as she hurried past.
Finally she was ushered into a room where five women received her
cordially. One of them said she could read, so Anna opened her
Bible to a chapter in Matthew and asked her to read it to the group.
She said, "I don't care for that. I want to read about prayer." And
turning to the others, she said, "Oh, they have beautiful supplica-

tions." She was shown the Lord's Prayer and said, "Oh, I know that," and proceeded to repeat it. Then it turned out that she had been a pupil briefly in a mission school years before and even in her Muslim environment had retained much of what she had learned. There were always some unexpected occurrences to disconcert the visitor. On the morning just described, Miss Thompson had begun to pray, when an old woman seated on the floor broke in loudly with the question, "Is that the direction of Mecca?" The house was near the river and a woman from a floor above let down a bucket and brought it up full of Nile water. As the bucket reached the level of the window where the visitor sat, one of the women with her reached out, pulled the bucket in, drank from it, and exchanged a few pleasantries with the neighbor leaning out above. No one was disturbed and only Miss Thompson was concerned about the filthy water.

One young missionary, just beginning to understand the language, told of a visit from Miss Thompson to her station and of going out with her to make calls—eleven of them! She wrote later, "I felt it was a privilege to be initiated into the work by one who has had so much experience and success." A favorite mission story is about a newcomer who became confused over Miss Thompson's procedures. Each time they approached a house Miss Anna Y would knock and wait patiently until a voice from inside called out, *"Meen?"* (Who?). She would give the traditional reply, *"Ana"* (I) and the woman would hurry to unbolt the door and welcome them in. It didn't seem to work so well when the new missionary tried this for herself, as she called out her own first name instead of the customary *"Ana,"* assuming that Miss Thompson had been doing the same.

One of the most valuable contributions Miss Thompson and her fellow workers made was in helping to break down the vicious mourning customs of the time. She told of going to see one poor woman who, after the death of a relative, had shown the depth of her grief by not going outside of her house for four years. A house of mourning was usually full of friends and neighbors for the first three days after a death and again on the fortieth day. In some cases the women covered their heads and clothing with mud or indigo, and would not continue their lessons with the Bible women or go out to church, as that would be considered a form of rejoicing.

At a funeral the men usually sat quietly in a tent on the street, drinking unsweetened coffee and listening to the chanting of the

Koran or prayers of a priest, depending on their faith. But the women kept up a continual wailing, urged on, if they should tire, by professional hired mourners. The house might be draped in black for months or even for a year, and this was true for Coptic families as well as Muslims. A well-to-do family owning a piano would close and lock it. The front room might be emptied of furniture so that mattresses could be placed around the walls. There every morning the women of the family and the neighborhood would sit by the hour, crying and reciting the virtues of the deceased. It was not unknown for a woman to lose her sight after weeks and months of this barbarous custom. Miss Thompson and her helpers often managed to bring a measure of sanity, at least temporarily, as they sat with such groups, reading words of comfort and praying with them. Sometimes the men of the house who had not been very welcoming previously would send special messengers to Miss Thompson, begging her and the Bible women to come and try to control the excesses of their women folk.

Of course a single visit could not accomplish this. In any case, since it was a visit of true sympathy and not merely the formal gesture expected at such a time, they would go again and again, trying to help the bereaved family conquer its grief. Miss Anna Y did not forget the individuals and the relationships involved and could draw upon her miraculous memory whenever she met any of the family again, to give another sympathetic word of help.

One day Miss Thompson went to a home where there had been a death just thirty-seven days earlier. There were ten women present, but she was acquainted with only two of the younger ones, who had been taking lessons. The women were resting after their first "round" of wailing, and coffee and cigarettes were being passed around. After a little chat Miss Thompson took out her Testament and was about to begin reading when one of the women stopped her. "Do not read now. This is not the time for it. We are mourning. After the forty days you may read." Miss Anna Y said later, "In earlier days I would have submitted quietly, but now I knew that defeat would have been inglorious to me, and women of that kind need to know the gospel. So, taking the principal talker by the hand, I said, 'Christ died and He died for us, and I am going to read some of His last words before He was crucified.' They listened attentively and told me that they considered me as their eyes, and were very cordial before I left them." So Anna went on climbing steep and dusty stairs for nearly sixty years, bringing hope to broken hearts.

This kind of work required a great deal of physical stamina, and sometimes sheer physical courage. Anna admitted that sometimes she was a little frightened when it was necessary for her to sleep in a village home. One morning in the Arabic church service all the women in the two rows behind the mission ladies jumped up and ran into the aisle, calling out that there was a scorpion. Mrs. Harvey caught sight of it crawling through their pew and was in time to put her foot on it. Its sting is extremely painful and can be fatal. The danger of disease was always present. Miss Thompson said that one day a woman came into her meeting carrying a child who obviously had the smallpox and she "felt a little timid." When cholera raged through the country, friends of the dying usually kept their distance, but not Miss Anna Y. When such a patient died in the hospital, just four people arrived for the funeral—the doctor, the Harveys and Anna Thompson. (Since the law in Egypt requires burial within twenty-four hours, the funerals are sometimes distressingly confused. At the death of a baby Miss Thompson put the poor child in the coffin, with ants running over and under the handkerchief over its face. Then one of the missionaries nailed the lid of the coffin down, using a chair rung in lieu of a hammer.)

Plain weariness was another problem. On trips to outlying stations Miss Anna Y tried to make the best use of her time. Once on a visit to Damanhur she said they had visited thirteen homes—"a full day and very pleasant." On a trip back to her first home in Egypt, Sinnoris, she received an overwhelming welcome, and casually commented that she had drunk twelve glasses of sweet sherbet and six cups of coffee that day. It didn't occur to her to avoid this health hazard by vague references to doctors' orders not to take anything between meals, as some missionary women were driven to do. (Some have been known to drop the rich feast cakes, so hospitably given, into their umbrellas when the hostess' attention had been momentarily distracted!) Miss Thompson did admit that she talked her throat dry some days, so perhaps the refreshments helped. In 1917, as she neared her sixty-seventh birthday, she counted up that she had called in six hundred and fifty-six Arab homes that year, in addition to many European homes, and attended countless meetings. By 1921 she was down to only five hundred and twenty-some houses!

During Miss Thompson's forty-seventh year on the field she wrote in the *Missionary Magazine* that sometimes she felt she was a little too rushed for a person her age, but as long as God gave her as much strength as she had, a desire for the work, and an increasing love for the people, she would not complain. She was distressed that she could not always make careful preparation, and that time for prayer was hard to preserve. She wrote, "There should be more time to spend on work for individuals, talking with inquirers, visiting them or praying with them, and more letters should be written to those who through their employment have been transferred to lonely places, or where there are no church privileges. This would be true also of church members, or former pupils, or hospital patients, no difference what their religion may be. It is a privilege to help direct the Egyptian workers and there should be more people who can be set apart for it. Those who meet educated Muslims should be well informed in the Muslim faith, but especially in bringing to their minds the right idea about our Saviour and the way of salvation. There seems to be an unlimited field open for visiting, and for beginning small meetings whether with the aid of a small school or without one. Much prayer is needed both here and at home for only God's Spirit can make these means effectual."

It was not easy to find mature women with enough education to teach the Bible in homes, who were free or willing to do such work. In early days several of the most faithful were blind women who carried their big Braille Bible portions with them as they found their way from house to house. As the number of workers in Cairo gradually increased, they developed specialties—one would be in great demand at mournings, another to settle quarrels. Reconciling antagonists was a large part of any day's work for the Bible women and for Miss Thompson and the other supervisors as well. One of the missionary societies made provision when it organized for one of its committees to be called, "Committee on Variance," i.e., a committee to patch up differences. Some of the Bible women were not very impressive to strangers, but Miss Thompson, while knowing their weaknesses, insisted they were God's favored ones, for she knew what they had to bear of weariness and often of insult.

One of the most faithful of Miss Anna Y's band of helpers was Sitt Bukhtea. Even in her old age she continued to work hard, often missing her noon meal entirely if there was a call to a mourning party or to pray with a sick person. She had an amusing habit of wearing several dresses at once under her *habera* or black robe. If she

was going on a trip, she seldom carried extra clothing—she simply
wore it. Once, as she came into a meeting where Miss Thompson
was, the latter was puzzled at an odd clinking sound Sitt Bukhtea
made as she walked. Later they discovered she was carrying a
half-dozen large empty bottles in the bloused back of her dress.
These were to be filled with eye medicine for her pupils. She was
utterly unselfish, giving away nearly everything she had. One day she
was helping a group of relatives off a train and was much occupied
with the young children. A man who had been seated near them
offered to help with one of the suitcases, and in the confusion he ran
off with it. Several days later, when Sitt Bukhtea was watching a
wedding procession from the balcony of the mission building, she
recognized the thief, who was made up like a clown and prancing
about at the head of the line. She ran down into the street, caught
hold of the man, and held on until a policeman came and heard the
story. They went to the man's house and found the suitcase. The
remarkable part of the story is that Sitt Bukhtea had only
one-quarter sight in one eye, and none in the other! She had been a
good student in the Ezbekieh school in her girlhood, but Miss
Thompson became concerned about her eyesight and persuaded her
to give up her English lessons. For a time she was a fine teacher in
the school, but it was as a Bible woman that she left her mark on
Cairo, especially in work among Muslims. She was tactful in
argument, but very persuasive. One day a man told her that he was
praying that God would help him get his son out of army
conscription, and if his prayer was answered as he asked he would
buy eighty Bibles to give away, and Sitt Bukhtea would be given half
of them to distribute. He kept his word and she was able to give
some of the Bibles to Muslims who came to her with questions about
her faith.

Superstition played a large part in the lives of the untaught
women whom the workers visited. Once Miss Thompson said she was
convinced that the conditions described in the Gospels where evil
spirits were in control of people also existed in some parts of Egypt's
society. Certainly many of the women believed in obsession and
they had elaborate rituals for casting out the spirits. A *sheikha*
would take a head kerchief from the afflicted person and put it
under her pillow, saying that the spirit responsible would appear to
her in the night. Identifying the spirit was supposed to help her to
determine the treatment needed. The patient would often be

suffering from lassitude, nausea, palpitation, and yawning. Miss Thompson knew two Coptic women who could not bear having the Bible read in their presence as it brought on epileptic fits. The ceremony of casting out a demon, known as holding a *zar*, required the payment of a fee and an invitation to all the friends who happened to have the same kind of demon. They dressed in white and seated themselves around a low table on which were placed various kinds of nuts and other food. To the accompaniment of drums the women chanted and swayed or danced about the room, giving the joy cry. Miss Anna Y once sat and watched three such rounds, left for a while, and returned to find them on the tenth round. A policeman came to inquire if they had obtained a permit for the *zar,* but the head of the house told Miss Thompson that it was a small thing, not requiring a permit, and the policeman was really looking for something to eat. The performance went on most of the night. Chickens were to be sacrificed the next day, though in a more serious case the *sheikha* would require the slaughter of a sheep. The patient would be ordered to ride the beast before it was killed. It was all very expensive, for the demon would demand jewelry, new dresses, etc. The whole scene was extremely weird and upsetting. Miss Thompson said she sometimes felt that modern Christians might be able to combat these beliefs if they really fulfilled Jesus' command about faith, prayer, and rigid self-denial.

At the time of Ahmed Fahmy's conversion one of his friends, a Muslim captain in the army, called on him at the mission. Later Miss Thompson and Abuna Michael went to call on him and his wife. Afterwards he came to the Arabic church service and accepted a New Testament gratefully, welcoming the suggestion that the mission ladies give lessons to his wife. But when Mrs. Lansing went to the house, she found the child was sick and the mother immediately accused her of putting the evil eye on the baby. She insisted that the only way to cure the child would be for Mrs. Lansing to give her a piece of her clothing, which would be burnt!

The Christian women, especially in the villages, had superstitions of their own, such as making the sign of the cross over the spot where a child had fallen and pouring on water and salt to make sure there would be no real injury. They had a custom of holding their palms up to receive the blessing when someone prayed, and then wiping them down their faces and clothing to apply the benefit. Almost all children wore some kind of charm, sometimes a great many. One day during a visit Miss Anna Y was puzzled by a large dark object hanging down a child's back. When she got close enough to see what it was, she was appalled to discover that it was the full-sized black hand of a mummy. The mother had lost several children and she was taking no chances with this one.

Many of the women had absorbed their husbands' attitude and decided that they were not capable of learning anything. Books were no help to women who could not read, and they had no contacts with the outside world. Sometimes an Egyptian teacher was not welcomed at first, and the missionary was able to provide an entrance for her since the stranger would be more respectfully listened to. Miss Smith said once that true, tender love and sympathy would go far in making the women willing to listen. She said, "The earnest worker will need zeal, courage, forbearance (she will need much of this), gentleness, tact, a thorough knowledge of the plan of salvation and how to tell it plainly, as to a little child, and a real appreciation of the preciousness of every soul with whom she comes in contact."

After solid months of this kind of exhausting work, the mission teachers learned that a break was necessary, not only for physical rest but to get a new perspective and perhaps new ideas. One missionary, though in China, not Egypt, wrote in the *Missionary Magazine,* "Though in splendid health, I do need, oh so much, to go home! I am soaked and saturated—not in heathenism, but in the type of character produced by centuries of heathenism. I should like to see what it would feel like to go a whole day without having a thought of suspicion or doubt about anyone around me; to take everything I hear said to me in the entire day for the face value of it without discounting a fraction of a percent; to have my own word taken in the same way, to feel that no one was weighing me in the balance." It is certain that Miss Anna Y never uttered so despairing a plaint, but she sometimes felt the drag of poverty and ignorance among the women she loved so well.

Miss Thompson got along well working with men, especially the Protestant pastors, all of whom she had known from their youth. But sometimes she grew exasperated with the attitudes of the church elders. In one village congregation the women had organized a little missionary society and collected a small offering, which they gave to the pastor to hold for them. But the elders thought it was entirely inappropriate for the women to presume to hold their own meetings.

They put on such pressure that the pastor had to return the money and persuade the women not to go on with their plans. Miss Thompson decided the men were simply afraid of any new thing. Occasionally they objected even to the pastor's meeting with the women, so she urged them to go ahead and meet alone. In some cases the problem was solved by finding a blind evangelist.

The women were quite used to sitting in a section of the church that was divided from the men's section by a wall or at least a curtain. Miss Thompson was distracted in one church to find herself behind a lattice screen. She said she was able to relax after she finally discovered that she could see the preacher if she kept one eye closed. But the women found ways to make a place for themselves after a while. They were studying their Bibles and joining the churches in greater numbers than the men, and in some cases they began to outnumber them. In one town where they wanted to organize a new congregation they were unable to find enough suitable men to serve as elders and they actually appointed a committee of women to act instead. When a man of that town applied for membership, the women, especially his wife, said he was not yet ready, and they deferred his acceptance!

In the case of Muslim women there was often great opposition from relatives to the idea of their being taught, more so than with the Copts. One woman who had learned to read and refused to quit reading the Bible was summarily divorced by her annoyed husband. A woman who became convinced of the truth of Christianity was not free to change her faith publicly—a girl was subject to the authority of her father, a wife to her husband's, and a widow to her eldest son's. Once in a while the shoe was on the other foot. One man wishing to be baptized was vehemently opposed by his wife, though she could not use the threat of divorce. Even single men had the greatest difficulty. A Muslim grocer in the Bulak section of Cairo was thrown out of his home when he decided to be baptized. He took a room elsewhere, but when he returned after the baptismal service he found his room had been rifled and everything destroyed. It was arranged that a policeman should go with him the next morning when he opened his shop. They found the door smeared with indigo, the sign of mourning, and with scrawled curses. A crowd tried to stone him and not even the police could protect him on the street. The students of the theological seminary offered to guard the shop in shifts and stay with him when he finally succeeded in reopening his place of business. Miss Thompson described how he decided to put a stop to the persecution after a gang of donkey boys began to curse him. He had the boys arrested, but when they begged for mercy at the police station, he asked the authorities to let them go. They demanded to know why he had complained if he did not want them punished. He said that he was taught by his faith to forgive and his only wish had been to help the police keep law and order in the city. The officials had a long talk with him, asking why he had changed his religion, and he went home beaming because he had had such an opportunity to witness for Christ.

Of course there were examples of Christians becoming Muslims, sometimes for very strange reasons. One young Copt, twenty years old, became engaged to a young woman his own age, but when the veil was lifted after the wedding ceremony he discovered a bride of seventy! When he raised an outcry, they insisted this was the woman he had contracted to marry, and the religious ceremony was binding. There was a great uproar about it, but Miss Thompson said that the only solution the family could find was conversion to Islam with freedom to divorce.

The band of home visitors continued to increase, little by little. Others of the mission staff were given supervision of certain districts of the city, but Miss Anna Y had over-all responsibility for the program. After Dr. Harvey's death in 1908, Miss Thompson and Mrs. Harvey remained in the same residence. Once a month all the women's workers met there for prayer and a Bible lesson, usually led by one of the pastors or the men of the mission. There were frequent courses in the theology of Islam and the way to explain the Christian faith to a Muslim inquirer. Dr. Samuel Zwemer, who was the best known of all the Islamic experts, occasionally gave special help to the Bible women on this subject. Miss Thompson took the reports of the nineteen women employed and kept track of the gifts they collected from the women for the sixteen missionary societies in the city. The number of pupils varied, but the total grew to over three thousand, usually about a fourth of the number being Muslims. Many of the latter came from the sections of the city where the mission was running small welfare clinics.

In order to improve the Bible women's knowledge and methods of work, the supervisors instituted an annual conference, which became a very popular occasion. They often reserved an entire third-class coach on the train, and groups got on board at each stop, to be joyfully welcomed by their friends from earlier stations. Miss Thompson usually had special responsibilities for these conferences. One year the committee assigned her a title for a talk, "The Message of the Teacher's Life," saying that no one had more right than she to be heard on the subject. Music was always an important part of the program, for the Bible women were frequently the only people in a meeting capable of leading the worship songs. One of the instructors said after one meeting that the tunes, when heard again, might not be exactly as they had been taught, for Egyptians had a way of "doctoring up" new tunes with various little twists and turns to suit their own fancy. However, the message would be the same, and that was the main thing. After a few years the missionaries began to feel that the meetings had become so cheery as to be almost frivolous, and not much serious work was being done. Hence the large conference was replaced by smaller area meetings where the group could sit about a table as a class and get down to hard study.

Although supervision of the home visitors took up a great deal of Miss Thompson's time, it was far from being her only evangelistic effort. All over the city there were tiny street Sunday schools and women's meetings, usually called missionary societies, which eventually became the nuclei of new Arabic congregations. Every day of the week there was a missionary society Miss Anna Y wanted to visit, but there weren't enough days. She was delighted when the societies became numerous enough to be organized into a presbyterial, and those annual meetings were a great pleasure to her. Just before her seventy-fifth birthday she traveled to Zagazig for a presbyterial meeting where she addressed a meeting of over four hundred women. The thank offering, modeled on the program of the American church, became a regular institution and she kept careful statistics of these gifts, made up of small but sacrificial contributions designated for the work of the church. Sometimes the Bible women brought in a few piasters to Miss Thompson to be put into the thank offering from their pupils and women who may not have been church members at all, but who wanted to share in the gift.

The most unusual contribution ever recorded in the Egyptian church was a baby. In the early years the collection plates were pans with handles. One communion Sabbath a woman asked Mrs. Harvey, "If one has a vow to the Lord, wouldn't this be a good time to pay it?" When assured that it would be, the woman lifted her baby, a few months old, and tried to put him into the pan. Mrs. Harvey managed to hold the pan and the baby, though taken by surprise, until the woman lifted the child back onto her lap. Twenty years later that boy entered the theological seminary.

In 1892 Miss Thompson reported seven missionary societies, three of them in Cairo, but there were seventy-four prayer meetings for women every week. As the local women began to take charge of the programs for the missionary societies, they suffered from a lack of program material in Arabic. This meant a great deal of translation from English by the missionaries, on top of their other duties, as well as considerable ingenuity in sparking original material. Miss Thompson thought that in general the programs prepared by the Egyptian women would do credit to any group. There were sometimes overseas visitors anxious to attend these meetings and occasionally they were able to make valuable contributions. The weekly meeting in Bulak welcomed two distinguished visitors one morning—Mrs. Lewis and her twin sister Mrs. Gibson, from Cambridge, England. Both spoke Arabic and gave short talks to the women. They were the women who discovered the Syriac manuscript of the New Testament at the monastery on Mt. Sinai and were then on their way to make a fourth visit to the monastery.

Miss Thompson's 1920 annual report states that there were seventeen street Sunday schools in operation in Cairo, with seven more to be started. One of these became Miss Anna Y's longest test of faith and endurance. It was located in a poor section of Bulak in the room hired for the little primary school. The children were dirty and unruly. They tried all kinds of tricks to disrupt the lesson, sometimes barking in unison like dogs. One afternoon a small girl arrived, leading a sheep, which she said she had to take care of, and if it couldn't stay she would have to leave too. They told her to stay and the antics of the sheep amused Miss Thompson almost as much as they did the children. The youngsters were crazy about the little Sunday school picture cards, whether they could read or not. They mobbed the teachers to get them, even out on the street, although they knew the cards were only for those who attended the Sunday school. One afternoon, when Miss Anna Y had made the mistake of taking some foreign visitors to the school, water was thrown all over them from the street. Week after week she wrote in her diary, "Children very naughty." Then one Sunday she arrived to find the landlady seated in the door with a stick to make sure no one entered. She had decided she would not rent the room any longer. Eventually another place was found, and they tried again. When the teacher blamed herself for not being able to control the children Miss Thompson said, "No, it was my fault. I slept this afternoon when I should have been praying for the school. I was not well prepared." But she was growing very tired.

Harassment was continual. One day the Bible woman was arrested because she was carrying her Bible under her arm—the Muslims arguing that this showed disrespect to a holy book! Nearly a hundred boys and girls were attending the little Sunday school by this time, and often Miss Anna Y, the Bible woman, and the evangelist were the only ones to control them. When they lost the help of the evangelist, it was decided that the school must close, after thirteen long years. Miss Thompson was in her late seventies by this time, but she had held on, hoping against hope that a church would take root. She said sadly that it was the only place in her missionary career where she had helped with a Sunday school or a women's meeting in which no permanent result would be seen. Perhaps she was wrong, however. One day, as she was riding through the city with one of the missionary doctors, their car was held up by a traffic light. A young lad came over to the car, opened the door, solemnly shook hands with Miss Thompson, closed the door again carefully, and stepped back. The doctor was naturally puzzled at this performance, until she explained that she had recognized him as one of the Muslim children who had attended her problem Sunday school. "He is one of my friends from Bulak," she said. And perhaps he remembered the stories of the Saviour as well as his teacher's kind face.

There was only one Egyptian pastor when Miss Thompson began her work, but when she celebrated her jubilee year there were sixty-three organized congregations in Egypt with eighty-five ordained ministers and seventeen thousand Sunday school pupils. Many of the small centers in Cairo had developed into full-fledged churches, which supported their pastors entirely. There were fourteen preaching places in the city of Cairo belonging to the Evangelical church. The main disappointment was that so small a percentage of the church members were converts from Islam.

But Miss Anna Y's sights were set far beyond the city limits. Her interest was fully as intense in the churches scattered over the country, and into the Sudan. She loved to attend the annual prayer conferences and meet old friends among the pastors and leaders. It was a happy day when she saw a good attendance of young people, and when the singing was enthusiastic. Sometimes the delegates traveled in a special railway car, and on one such trip they began to sing. As the car rolled into Cairo's main station, everyone on the platform hurried to see what was happening. Miss Anna Y said the old Psalms never sounded so good.

One of Miss Thompson's adventures occurred when she traveled to Minia, several hours south of Cairo, for a prayer conference. A convention of cotton merchants was being held at the same time and the hotels were full. By some misunderstanding no arrangements had been made for Miss Anna Y and for two of the men of the mission who arrived with her just after midnight. When they were turned away from the one really comfortable hotel, they tried a less desirable one a few blocks away, but that too was full and the manager directed them to a kind of boarding house not far away. There the man in charge assured them he would have rooms for them right away. Nothing happened. They sat and waited. When they made further inquiries he told them they would be cared for without delay. A few minutes later a man staggered into the lobby, still half-asleep and obviously dressed in a hurry after a rude awakening. The manager went to the three weary missionaries and said with a grand gesture, "The room is ready for the lady now." She didn't turn it down, as there was obviously no other choice.

At one of the prayer conferences they had arranged a program they thought would attract Muslims, but very few turned up. When Dr. Samuel Zwemer arrived, and it was time for his address, the Muslims arrived too. He was the one person they had heard about and were curious to see. Sometimes the program was devoted almost entirely to prayer. At the closing session of one such conference a young pastor led in a very moving and humble prayer that God would take his life and use it in any way He chose. There were tears in Miss Thompson's eyes when he finished. After the benediction she leaned over to the younger missionary beside her and said, "If that young man really meant what he said, this evening can be one of the most important sessions we have ever had." He has since become probably the leading preacher of his generation in Egypt.

The missionaries were sometimes accused of concentrating on educating the Orthodox Coptic Christians in their own faith rather than tackling the harder job of reaching Muslims. This was always a matter of great concern to Miss Anna Y. She was interested in everyone, from the house servant to the high government official. She told of going to a precommunion service in Ramleh in 1894 where she found among the men in attendance a sheikh from the local mosque. He was actually a descendant of the famous Sayyid el Badawi. But he had become interested in Christianity and had bought about sixty Christian books. The day after the church service he took several of the men he had met there and showed them the mosque, actually leading them up into the minaret. Though Miss Thompson had no opportunity to talk with that particular man, she did make her own opportunities in a great many ways. For a long while she went down to the front door of the mission building and sat on a bench under the stairs with the Muslim doorkeeper, reading the Bible with him and teaching him to read it for himself. He asked for his own Bible and she got him a large one with all the vowels included to make it easier for him. He was doing well until the men missionaries laid down the law—it was not appropriate for a lady to sit with the servant, and she was to stop it. So they sent a thirteen-year-old boy to teach the doorman and Anna lost her pupil. She took this disappointment very hard, but she could still pray for him and let him see she was interested in his progress. He was one of God's children, as precious as any other to Miss Anna Y. He was one of a great many thousands she sat with to speak of her Saviour during her long years of evangelistic work.

CHAPTER V

SIDELINES

From the days of her first ocean crossing to the end of her life, Anna Thompson's music wove a bright thread through all of her days. Of course, the church songs were her great love; but one could not be really surprised to see a little handwritten note drop out of a record book and discover it to be the words of "Oh, the bullfrog on the bank!" When young people visited Mrs. Harvey's hospitable home in Cairo, as British soldiers—about forty of them—did regularly on Friday evenings, there was always music. The diaries often note, "Singing downstairs at 7:00." Miss Anna Y's expense sheet shows money orders sent to the States for music books and games to use on those evenings. A letter from Scotland once brought an interesting story of one of the songs used with the soldiers. A visitor to Miss Thompson's group sang it as a solo with an accompaniment arranged by a Scottish regimental bandmaster. People were so taken with the words that they hunted up the authoress in Britain, and she in turn, delighted at the poem's acceptance in Egypt, wrote to ask for the music and the name of its composer.

Miss Anna Y was very faithful in teaching her schoolgirls to sing, as well as the pupils in the boys' school and the theological students, even more than mature Bible women. Her report of the attendance at a church service was likely to mention the music, such as on one evening when they had "one bass present." He turned out to be a man from the United States naval vessel *Gettysburg.* Her most loyal disciple in this crusade was one of the theological students, Rev.

Ghobriel Rasqalla, who became the pastor of the Ezbekieh congregation. It was he who organized the first choir to introduce the church book of Psalms at the annual prayer conference in 1917 in Zeitun, a few miles outside of Cairo. The choir consisted of four Egyptian men, one of the men missionaries, and Anna Thompson. In the years that followed, Pastor Ghobriel organized and trained a large mixed choir that ventured into church anthems and set the pattern which other congregations followed.

As early as 1894 Miss Anna Y recorded that she had begun to write down tunes in the sol-fa system. In January of 1896 she was one of a group appointed to choose new psalter tunes, and throughout the following June and July her diaries mention all-day meetings of the music committee of the association. Again in 1912 she began meeting with a psalmody committee assigned to revise the church Psalm book. Much of what should have been a summer vacation went into this work, as they met first at Schutz near Alexandria and through July and September in Cairo. In November they were at work in Assiut and again in January. The special section on tunes met again that month in Beni Suef, south of Cairo. By March they were trying out some of the new arrangements in the churches, but the work of the committee continued. In January, 1916, the committee made its report. They had spent four years, choosing and adapting 237 tunes, 66 of them Oriental. The year's budget for the hard-working committee was all of $300. Ten years later some of the results of their work were visible in the excellent music at the annual prayer conference when Pastor Ghobriel led the choir. Miss Thompson said he had had a great deal to do with the versifying of the new Psalm version, as well as in the selection of tunes.

In the small edition, printed with both music and words, that was used in playing the reed organs or pianos in many Arabic churches, Westerners were distracted by the backwards settings of the tunes. The publication committee had decided that since the Arabic words read from right to left, the music should go that way too. With the accidentals on the wrong side of the notes and everything completely backwards, it took some time for the musicians to be able to read the often familiar music. For Westerners the Oriental tunes, almost always minor and wandering, presented difficulties of their own, but naturally they were the most popular with the congregations.

It was a great occasion for Miss Thompson when Dr. Ira B. Sankcy visited Cairo in 1898. She was one of the welcoming committee at the station and had the pleasure of entertaining him and his wife in the home she shared with Mrs. Harvey. The next morning Dr. Sankey attended the Arabic service at the church in the Bulak area and sang for the congregation. Years later Homer Rodeheaver was her guest and sang for the schoolchildren in the Ezbekieh auditorium. He also "played tunes on his instrument," as Miss Thompson put it.

Evening services in the Egyptian congregations often finished with a song fest. One night in Assiut, when they had gone on rather late, Miss Anna Y told friends with amusement that she had had an escort back to her residence—ten men! Many of the same group gathered a few nights later in the home of one of the well-to-do Protestant church members. In saying a reluctant goodnight at the close of another musical evening, their host asked if they would please "leave their voices behind."

It was as an Arabic expert that Miss Thompson made another significant contribution to the work in Egypt. She had a good ear and a phenomenal memory so that she was able very quickly to carry her end of an Arabic conversation. There are certain "compliments" or traditional phrases and responses that are expected of one, either as host or guest, in an Egyptian home—a major pitfall for many beginners—and she was able to master these rapidly. Her pronunciation was exact so that her reading of the Arabic Bible was acceptable wherever she went, and her prayers were moving rather than distracting as are those of so many poorly equipped Westerners. The mission soon recognized her special gifts and put her to work on the language committee of the association. This was a time-consuming and wearying task, but she never complained. Over and over again her holiday time in the summer went into day-long Arabic examinations for new missionaries, with other days to follow of paper-grading and preparing reports for the association. No quaking beginner was ever bullied by Miss Anna Y. Although she had not experienced the severe difficulties many of them suffered in trying to learn the language, she was always quietly sympathetic and gave them what confidence she could.

However, a major disagreement later brought her to request the association to relieve her of this assignment. She could not approve the committee's policy in separating the colloquial Arabic from the

classical, and in preparing textbooks in phonetic script for the
spoken language. It was all one to her, and she thought such a
division was quite unnecessary and harmful. Her first request to
resign was not accepted because the association did not want to lose
her valuable help, but eventually she did succeed in withdrawing. To
the end of her life she did not change her opinion in this matter.
Neither could she see the point in the grammatical approach to the
language which the new textbooks offered. One evening one of the
young language students, completely bewildered over the rules
governing "weak" verbs, went to Miss Thompson's room and begged
for help. She took one look at the book and shook her head. "I'm
no help at all with this," she said. "I didn't learn Arabic that way.
You should learn it by listening, hearing how the people talk. You
need to get the feel of it. All these rules won't help. And it's
ridiculous to make a second language out of the colloquial. I disagree
with these phonetic scripts entirely."

Another aspect of Miss Anna Y's varied interests was her
sympathy for the British soldiers in the city. Dr. Andrew Watson in
his book, *The American Mission in Egypt* (1897), wrote: "Since the
Arabi rebellion the need of English services in Presbyterian forms
became more pressing. Soon after the British troops entered the city
many of them called on the missionaries. . . . Arrangements were
made by the Presbyterian chaplain to the British forces and the
missionaries to have a parade service of the 42nd Highland Regiment
held in the Mission church. . . . It was a grand sight to see those
strong-bodied Highlanders, in their parade kilts, march into the
church, and when they joined in singing the 23rd Psalm or the 100th
or some other well-known Psalm the sound was like the resounding
sea. A weekly union prayer meeting was started in July, 1883, in
Mrs. Harvey's parlor. . . . She has left her parlor open for Christian
soldiers all these years, and she, Miss Thompson, and others have had
a good influence over them."

Almost every Sunday evening there would be a dozen or more of
these men and of other British units at the family dinner table after
church, sometimes after another large group had been served tea in
the afternoon. One Sabbath, Anna listed twenty-eight soldiers as
dinner guests. One drunk man came in for the singing and had
delirium tremens on the spot. One New Year's Day Miss Thompson
said she and Dr. Harvey had held open house all day long, except
when he was out making fourteen calls! Every Tuesday evening she

went to the YMCA where many of the soldiers showed up, and every
Friday evening the house was given up to their entertainment. Mrs.
Harvey usually picked up her knitting—she made innumerable pairs
of bootees for all new babies—and Miss Thompson led in the games
and singing. The friendships formed were often kept up by letter,
and on furlough voyages Miss Anna Y made a point of seeing old
friends at the Gibraltar stop or in Britain.

But home entertainment was not enough. Over and over the notes
tell of going to the Continental Hotel to help entertain wounded
soldiers (in 1915); of going to the hospital in Kasr el Aini barracks,
where she spread eighty loaves of bread at a party for over four
hundred soldiers; of continual serving in "tea rooms" for the men; of
At Homes for army nurses; of a tea for six hundred soldiers and
nurses where Lord Radstock made a speech; of pouring tea for the
soldiers at the YMCA; of helping with a tea for six thousand men in
the Ezbekieh Gardens—"the other American ladies were outside, but
I was inside on the skating rink." All of this beyond her regular
mission work makes it not very surprising that she commented, "Not
very spry today" in her sixty-seventh year. But almost the next day
she gave supper to forty or forty-five delegates to the Bible Women's
Conference. In 1917 the common report was, "Eighteen for supper
and ten more came in for singing afterwards." At this time, too, Mrs.
Harvey was ill in the hospital for many months, and in addition to
visiting her every day Miss Thompson was carrying all the responsibility of the home alone. She kept on month after month going to
the canteens "spreading bread" for a YMCA tea for three thousand
men, or another given by Governor Allenby for five hundred
convalescent soldiers in the Garden; visiting the hospitals to read to
the men; even making aprons for the hospital orderlies. It was no
wonder that the diary carried a big underlined notation on the day
when she could write, "PEACE SIGNED."

The soldiers had a great deal of sympathy from these devoted
women, although the latter suffered on account of the men's
behavior sometimes. When the Australian soldiers attacked the
red-light district not far. behind the mission building, burning and
destroying the area because of their anger at being "rolled" and
stolen from, it did not surprise Miss Anna Y and Mrs. Harvey. One
day two soldiers came to the house, saying they were hungry. It was
obvious they had spent all their money on liquor, but they were
taken in and given a good meal. A certain British officer was told
that he had the most orderly company in the regiment. He said, "I

told them if I had, it was because of the influence of the American missionaries." Young men far from home and in the midst of degrading surroundings found new strength in that home of prayer and good fun.

Besides the soldiers, hospitality went to a wide range of other visitors, some coming to Egypt in the vain hope of finding health, and some of great fame. Miss Thompson met hundreds of them at the railway station, helping many who were very ill when they arrived, and enjoying the friendship of the many distinguished men and women who found their way to Cairo. She called on Lady Cromer and Mrs. Keith Falconer while they were staying near the mission in the 1880's. She and Mrs. Watson talked with Mrs. Helen Gould Shepheard at her hotel one day in 1915. Later it was Mrs. Shepheard's generosity that made it possible for dozens of young Egyptian boys and girls to be given Bibles as prizes for memorization of long passages of Scripture. A few days after seeing Mrs. Shepheard, it was Miss Jane Addams of Chicago who entertained Miss Thompson to tea. She herself had the pleasure of entertaining many well-known people like Dr. John R. Mott, Dr. Sherwood Eddy, and Dr. Francis E. Clark, and she was much involved in helping to arrange their speaking programs while in Egypt. She was invited to the British Residency one day with Mrs. Harvey and commented only, "The Duke of Connaught there, and the Sultan, etc."

In April of 1924 the *Franconia* brought seven hundred tourists to Egypt and many of them visited the mission building in Ezbekieh. (Unfortunately, seventy-five members of the tour developed ptomaine poisoning, although staying at Shepheard's, considered the best hotel in the city.) Sometime later a large party organized by the *Christian Herald* arrived, including Dr. and Mrs. Charles M. Sheldon, and again Miss Thompson was in the welcoming party. She took twenty of the visitors to see the Girls' College while others of the mission staff guided one hundred and sixty of the group on a bus tour of the work of the mission. When "Pussyfoot" Johnson arrived, and addressed a meeting at the YMCA, Miss Anna Y was greatly amused that the crowd had quietly dissolved before the chairman could move a vote of thanks. At a tea given for the American ambassador, Anna was finally introduced to Saad Pacha Zaghlul, only a few weeks before his death.

There is no way of knowing how many lonely and needy foreign visitors were discovered and cared for by this indefatigable meeter of trains and visitor of hospitals. Cairo doctors were exasperated at the way British doctors advised their patients to go to Egypt for the winter, forgetting that the dust would be more harmful to weak lungs than would the misty weather of Britain. One specialist said that when such patients showed up at his office his only advice was to buy a ticket on the first boat home. Many such sufferers were comforted by visits from Miss Thompson as soon as she heard of them. Some, who had arrived in the hope of finding health, found death instead. In a "good" winter Cooke and Son reported that in one month they had the sad duty of shipping home the bodies of seven persons who had died. One cannot guess how many were cared for when the weather was unfavorable.

Since Miss Thompson was the youngest of the elderly women missionaries in the Ezbekieh building, it became her duty to run the errands and take charge of things generally. The house was always in demand as a kind of missionary hotel, so housekeeping was a demanding chore. One day Anna remarked that she had not cleaned the guest room very well, for they had had three sets of guests in twenty-four hours. One morning she was up at five o'clock to see about breakfast for a party of five leaving on the early train, later going to the station to see them off. She remarked a little ruefully that nothing had been said about board. The members of the mission had a standing arrangement to contribute a fixed amount for each day they availed themselves of the hospitality of a mission home in another station. However, these were guests from another mission and evidently they were not aware how much their five-day stay had strained the small budget of the household. But in addition to housekeeping, Miss Thompson found a great many more interesting things to do, such as attending the flower show or the Queen's birthday review; visiting the King Tut exhibit at the museum; hearing addresses by the archeologists Sir Flinders Petrie and Dr. Breasted, or by Sir William Wilcox, builder of the first Assuan dam, or by Labrador's Dr. Grenfell. At the regular monthly At Home in their own household it was common to receive seventy-five or eighty people in an afternoon.

No one was more interested than Miss Anna Y in the accomplishments of missions and churches other than her own. The Anglican bishop's prayer meeting was a monthly appointment she rarely missed, and she enjoyed it, although she complained that "only men

prayed." A Coptic bazaar or a union prayer meeting of thanksgiving
for the deliverance of Jerusalem would find her on hand. After one
inter-mission meeting in Ramleh in 1899 she went with a group to
Abukir to see where the other missionaries were spending their
holidays. She found one tent, where some Pentecostal missionaries
were living, which had the text, "Have ye received the Holy Ghost
since ye believed?" stretched around the doorway. That kind of
approach was never Miss Thompson's style.

In the first recorded minutes of the mission association meetings
after Anna reached Egypt her name appeared only with occasional
statistical reports, requests for leave, or for additional help. After the
women were admitted to the meetings, it is common to find her
name as one who had been asked to close a session with prayer, or
serve as one of a committee to prepare a memorial to a member of
the mission who had died. (They seemed to think this was something
she could do very well.) But after her many abilities became
apparent, she was given a number of important committee assignments. In addition to the music and language committee duties
already mentioned, she was called upon to share in the long
deliberations concerning the best use for a special gift for "forward
work." Dr. G. Campbell White of New York suggested that prayer
circles be formed at home, and it became Miss Thompson's duty to
send him requests for prayer from all the stations, to be published
each month. She served for a time on the committees that supervised
the girls' orphanage and the Tanta Hospital, as well as on the
Location Committee that assigned the missionaries to the various
stations and areas of work. A special committee was set up for
women's work, consisting of three single women and three mission
wives, of which she was a member. It was her regular assignment to
send news items to the denominational weekly, *The United
Presbyterian.* She was a member of the Sudan Committee, the
World's Sunday School Committee, and many others, several of
them simultaneously. Sometimes her wisdom was called upon in
property matters. When a congregation in Bulak asked for land to
build a church building, she was on the deliberating committee.
Their decision was that "when the congregation had raised the
funds to build a building, a small plot would be ceded to them for as
long as they follow the same faith and practices of worship as the
Synod. If defection shall occur (which God forbid) the property to
revert to the Board."

One of Miss Anna Y's special interests was the Women's Christian Temperance Union. She saw to it that the schools she supervised had temperance societies as well as missionary societies, and she labored long and hard to start an Arabic branch of the union in Cairo. There was an English-speaking group there as early as 1891, begun by Mrs. Mary Clement Leavitt, and Miss Thompson put on her white ribbon and became a faithful member. Some of the wealthier Protestant women began to take a deep interest in the organization and invited the group to meet in their homes. They were very encouraged when Saad Zaghlul's wife began to attend. Of course, Islamic teaching was entirely in favor of this particular program, and they had hopes of real government backing. It was not until 1923 that the Arabic society was finally organized with forty members. By the following winter they could report that there were a great many important Muslim ladies attending. Miss Mary J. Campbell, who had done much for the temperance cause in India, arrived in Egypt in 1925 for a visit. Meetings were arranged for her in various parts of the country. Miss Thompson went with her to call on the famous Russell Pacha, who did so much to control the international drug traffic. He was very cordial, discussing at length the government's plan for controlling the cocaine problem in Egypt. Four years later the British temperance leader, Miss Agnes Slack, visited Cairo, and again Miss Thompson was involved in the arrangements, including a large public meeting at the American University.

It distressed Miss Anna Y that in a country where the government and the official religion were against drinking, it should be the foreigners and the Christians who set the bad example. Many who were anxious to imitate Westerners felt that liquor was a part of that life. Miss Thompson depended on temperance literature to help in the WCTU program and was pleased when part of the thank offering from the women's meetings was designated for its publication. She would get requests from Muslim friends, railway officials, and others for Arabic leaflets they could enclose in letters to their friends. The schoolchildren were supplied with leaflets to take home, and school dialogues frequently included instruction on the evil of intemperance.

The government had forbidden the growing of hemp, from which hashish is made, as early as 1884. Importation was also forbidden, with very high penalties attached. In 1904 a law was passed forbidding the public smoking of hashish, but many ways were found to evade it. The manufacture of alcoholic drinks was governed by the "Law on Inconvenient, Unhealthy and Dangerous Establishments." Import duties were high and the government, through the help of a Christian official, tried to reduce the number of selling licenses, but again there was much evasion of the law. Sniffing hashish and cocaine became a great curse to the country during the 1920's and smuggling was a big industry. Some of the worst offenders were protected by the capitulations that exempted foreigners from arrest under Egyptian law. A favorite crop in Upper Egypt was the poppy, and women often gave a distillation of the pods to their babies to keep them from crying and make them sleep. The government outlawed the cultivation of poppies, but it was only when airplanes became available that it was possible to find the plots hidden within fields of grain.

Miss Thompson served as the very faithful president of the Cairo branch of the WCTU for thirty-six years. By the time of her death there was a flourishing national organization in Egypt with other fine leaders. She had had the privilege of attending a world convention of the union in London and was much impressed by Miss Frances Willard. It was not an entirely happy occasion for her, however. She was not used to British reserve and her natural friendliness met with less response than usual, so that she admitted she felt a little lonely and snubbed, but she enjoyed the meetings and eventually made some fine new friends.

As Miss Thompson became better known in Egypt and abroad she was asked to represent the mission at several large gatherings. In 1901 she attended the Des Moines meeting of the United Presbyterian General Assembly and the Women's General Missionary Society in Monmouth, Illinois. Traveling on to Portland, she was impressed anew with the fact that her family had made that difficult journey so many years before. "How did father ever take us across this terrible desert?" she asked herself. Meeting her sister, she went on to San Francisco to an Epworth League convention. This was a great occasion, with the city illuminated and messages not only from the governor but from the President of the United States.

An even more impressive occasion came in 1910 when Miss Anna Y was appointed a delegate from Egypt for the great International Missionary Conference in Edinburgh. All the great personalities in missions were there and policies were laid down that influenced missionary programs for fifty years and more. In reporting the opening meeting at St. Giles church, she quoted the Scripture reference and the text of the sermon, mentioned the immense crowd, and then, true to her nature, added, "Fine music," before she noted that Lord Balfour took the chair for the next session. Her very full notes are a treasury of mission history.

Late in 1914, at the invitation of the Sudan Mission Association and by appointment of her own mission, Miss Thompson made an official visit to the work in the Sudan. All along the way, as her train stopped at various stations, she was greeted by friends and fellow workers, sometimes bearing tea and food. She stopped in Aswan for one day and managed to visit the Christian Endeavor Society and five homes. On January 3 she was met in Khartum by the American missionaries and "Odoke with his fancy hair." For the next nine days she sat with the association in annual meeting and visited various mission projects. It was a wonderful experience for her and for her hosts, who wrote a most appreciative letter of thanks to the Egyptian association for her helpful visit.

Once again in 1920 Miss Anna Y represented the mission at the Topeka General Assembly, and then shared the spotlight with other missionaries at the Women's General Missionary Society meeting in Youngstown, Ohio. She attended the conference in New Wilmington, Pennsylvania, where she was presented with a gold watch, and then for several weeks she kept a strenuous speaking schedule in the Muskingum, Ohio, presbyterial. She received gifts amounting to $152, so she gave $135 to the girls' orphanage in Cairo and spent $17 to have a good photograph made of herself. This was to be given to the churches that had been supporting her work for thirty-five years. Moving on to the Pittsburgh area, she continued to report to the women's societies about the work in which they were so interested. One Sunday she spoke to two classes and then to an entire Sunday school in the morning. In the afternoon she spoke to the mission circle named for her, and then to the students at the theological seminary. In the evening she spoke at the First United Presbyterian church service. She listed fifteen major addresses between September 19 and October 7. The ladies of the women's board held a reception for her. As they had learned, along with many others, that it was useless to send money to Miss Anna Y to be spent on herself, they had presented her with a new black satin dress, which she described as "very fine" and which she wore to the reception. The president of the board took off her own coat and put it on Miss Thompson, so she felt really dressed up for once.

Among all the activities that engaged Miss Anna Y's attention, there emerges another major concern—the place of women. She was not a feminist and did not rebel at any of the decisions made for her by the men in her family or in the mission, but she understood that Egyptian society and especially the church could not advance faster than its women folk. She struggled to help them feel their own worth and potential, refusing to let them sigh and give up in the face of criticism and frustration. She realized that the young pastors needed educated wives and she was delighted when one of them chose a graduate of the school, even giving up valued teachers in the same spirit. Her opinion was that a minister's wife in Egypt held an even more important position than one in the States. She must set the standard in the village church by her housekeeping, her care of the children, and in defying old superstitions and customs, just as her husband would set an example in the town on the strength of his general education and his ability to lead the religious life of his people. Theirs might well be the only home of educated people in a whole village.

In an article Miss Thompson wrote for the *Moslem World* in 1927 she said that the minds of men in Egypt had been in great commotion over the question of allowing women to remove their veils. Some of the younger men felt it was time for this and they formed a society to push the matter. One of this group pretended to want to enroll his sister as a pupil in a nuns' school, and took advantage of his admission into the building to address the students. He urged them to refuse to wear the veil, much to the dismay of the traditionalists among the parents. The young men tried this same tactic in some of the mission schools but were prevented from disrupting classes there.

A young Egyptian studying in England wrote to the Muslim press that the men blamed the women for their ignorance when the men themselves were responsible for it. He described the education available to girls in England and said there was no danger in it. In fact, he said, a rich girl enjoys many advantages from it and a poor girl is able to earn a living without having to support herself by vice. A Turkish paper at this time insisted that the East would not be elevated until woman was elevated, adding, "The fall of Muslim womanhood has been the greatest reason for the fall of the whole nation." Some felt that removing the veil would not solve the situation but would encourage Muslim women to copy frivolous Westerners and flirt with men. Others said the Koran did not command the veil; it originated with the wealthy and was later given religious sanction. Country women have always moved about freely, many without the veil, and no one considers them less virtuous than others. Another student wrote passionately, "Do you believe that honor which can only be protected by a rag on the face is an honor preserved? You fill the world shouting out that freedom is the natural right of man. But when one of your arms is extended with prayer and supplication for freedom and dustour (a constitution) and with the other you press upon your daughter, wife, sister, and mother with a palm of flint and fingers of iron, they know that your clamoring after freedom and your tears for the dustour are only a mockery."

The Egyptian government began to send a few girls abroad for better education on the condition that they would teach for a certain length of time on their return to Egypt. Miss Thompson reported that one Muslim woman brought an action against the government because her teaching had made her lose the opportunity of getting married. Even in the 1920's young women taking teaching positions in the mission schools were facing this old problem, since many people still assumed that these women were not from good families.

In 1911 Miss Thompson prepared a paper, one of many articles from her pen, for the Lucknow Conference on Work Among Muslims. It was published in *Daylight in the Harem,* which was edited by Dr. Samuel Zwemer and Miss Annie Van Sommer. The paper was entitled, "Reform in Egypt." She described how some Muslim women boasted to her that they could not read in the same way they boasted of being kept at home by husbands as

an evidence that their husbands appreciate them and don't want them to be seen by the common crowds. That attitude belongs in the past. However, there is still a long way to go, for a man of position in Cairo has just proposed a scheme for educating Egyptian girls which requires the avoidance of foreign influence, wearing the veil and robe, being given only an elementary education and leaving school before they reach the age of thirteen. An evolution is going on. The veil is often so thin as to be only an enhancement. Women may go out to shop or for visits without being accompanied by a eunuch or a servant. The marriageable age has been raised so that in Cairo a girl is seldom married under twelve. Plurality of wives is slowly going out of fashion among the educated classes but is still common among wealthy village men.

Women of position are beginning to organize in Cairo to improve the place of women and collect money for public charities. Some of them have become fervent nationalists, generally following their husbands' views in politics as in religion.

Primary schools for girls should be greatly increased so that they can read and write Arabic, learn the principles of religion and morality, and a little sewing.

There is feverish excitement as if the Muslims were afraid of losing their religion and thinking that the government must be called upon to help them retain it. But there is a willingness to listen to Christian teaching, more than ever before, with a greater desire for education in Christian schools.

Miss Thompson was asked to serve on the Continuation Committee of the Lucknow Conference in an effort to furnish literature to Muslim women. She lived to see the day when the above quotation was definitely out of date, but she still saw great goals ahead.

Of all the projects Miss Anna Y cherished, many people felt that the Christian Endeavor Society was closest to her heart. The young men who gathered in her drawing room were of all denominations and nationalities, including at times a large number of British soldiers. It seemed more appropriate to link it with a world organization than with the young people's organization of her own church. At first it was a kind of debating society, meant for discussion but barring politics. Miss Thompson was much concerned about the young men from Upper Egypt who were coming to Cairo to attend the higher schools of law, medicine, engineering, agriculture, etc. Obviously this opportunity for them to practice their English was a great attraction for these bright young men initially, but they became much involved in the society and attended loyally for years. Some of them later were very prominent in the political life of Egypt and helped to shape its new constitution. Miss Anna Y was unhappy about the rumors of political deals she heard these boys of hers were engaged in years later, but she had faith that their early Christian training would determine their direction in the final analysis.

A letter from Mrs. Harvey to the *Missionary Magazine* in 1900 said, "There were twenty-five present at our C. E. meeting last evening. Among them were eight Americans, two Scotch, four English, one Welsh, three Italians, two Armenians and four Egyptians, but all understanding the English language. These meetings have been a blessing to many. Often we have letters read from those who have met with us but are now far away."

Miss Thompson was a faithful member of the large Christian Endeavor group that met in the prayer room of the Ezbekieh building on Sunday afternoons for a great many years. She felt responsible for the meeting, and if there was a pause, she was likely to nudge the person next to her and say, "Get up and pray." One of the mission men told once of an interesting encounter at this meeting during his first weeks in Egypt. He noticed two young Egyptians among the group of Englishmen and Americans who were present and felt sorry for them, thinking they had got into the meeting by mistake and were too polite to leave although they probably could understand little of what was going on. The minute the meeting closed, Miss Thompson went to them and shook hands, then called the young missionary over to meet them. To his surprise, they spoke excellent English. They were law students at the government school and said they were Muslims but had enjoyed the meeting very much. Miss Thompson tactfully suggested that they might be glad to call on the missionary at his home. The idea had not entered his head, but all he could do was to say that he would be glad to see them.

They showed up the very next evening. They were full of enthusiasm for the independence of Egypt and the American felt out of his depth as he had not learned much about local politics at that stage. He had got the idea from some source that he would be going out as a missionary to a run-down and decadent race; that the outstanding defect in the Egyptian character was lack of ambition. The nationalist demonstrations he saw immediately after his arrival gave this impression a severe jolt. These two young callers certainly had enthusiasm, and he decided this was something that a good missionary ought to capture for Christ.

They were full of questions about America and finally said they would like to study the New Testament because they wanted to broaden their education and understanding of Christian nations. He told them that if they studied the New Testament together, he would not try to force his beliefs on them, but his motive would be to lead them to accept Jesus as the Son of God and their Saviour. They agreed on that understanding and studied one evening a week for nearly a year, bringing three others of their friends to join the group. Two of them went to Europe for further study and one wrote back, "I am seeking the truth in religion and I desire to follow it even though it may mean giving up my faith in Muhammed." No one knows the outcome of that year's contacts, but none of it would have come to pass if Miss Thompson had not quietly maneuvered to bring the young men together.

A year or so later Miss Thompson wrote about the Saturday night group: "Tonight there was a very pleasant Christian Endeavor social for our Saturday evening meeting of young Egyptians. There were thirty-one of them, if we count two Syrians in government employ as belonging to this country. Three or four were Muhammedans who are much enlightened and who enjoy attending the meeting. Some of these young men are in the War Department and have served for longer or shorter times in the Sudan. One is employed in the Observatory, one in the Public Works, some in the telegraph and post office, while the largest number are in the railway department of government service. So all are educated young men and English is the language used."

On the occasion of Miss Thompson's seventy-eighth birthday the Egyptian Christian Endeavor members and alumni gave a dinner for her at the Central YMCA. A *bey*, a prominent lawyer, sat on her right, and a judge, later knighted by the British government, on her left. There were speeches, telegrams arrived from all over the country, and she was presented with a beautiful clock and other gifts. But she hadn't given up her work for the C.E. yet. A few days later she attended the first Christian Endeavor convention held in the Ezbekieh church. (There were numerous societies by this time, many of them in the schools, some of which Miss Anna Y had organized.) Her only comment on the program was, "Rev. Ghobriel's choir did wonders." The meeting went on all day and she felt the attention and enthusiasm were splendid.

It was a disappointment to her that the younger missionaries did not pick up her enthusiasm. There was a standing invitation to go with her to the Sunday-afternoon meeting, where many young women now attended along with the men. But the language students felt that an Arabic service in the morning, sometimes involving teaching a Sunday school class, playing the organ for the service, etc., with choir practice and English service in the evening, were all they could manage on a so-called day of rest. Miss Thompson tried a special strategy of calling on some of the short-term teachers in the Ezbekieh building on Sunday afternoons and then inviting them to go with her when it came time for the C. E. meeting. But if necessary she often went alone, and with unflagging interest, at nearly eighty years of age.

This was equally true of her other "sidelines"—music, Arabic, politics, temperance work, ecumenical contacts, women's place in society, and the church. She never grew weary in spirit; only the flesh grew weak.

CHAPTER VI

LIFE WITH A GLOW

How can one sum up Anna Y. Thompson as a person?—frugal yet wildly generous, humble but unashamedly pleased with a compliment, old-fashioned in her dress and manner but tolerant of others, firm in her insistence on woman's place but often disapproving of her sex, usually unwilling to criticize but at times frankly outspoken. She was a complex individual, but loved and respected by thousands.

Miss Anna Y had a rich sense of humor that was never cruel and was often directed at herself. One day a party on a boat ride ran into rough weather and many of the group grew frightened. Miss Thompson called out, "Don't be afraid! The boat is only going over." Joining in the laugh, she admitted that that wasn't exactly what she had meant to say. She used to say ruefully, "Figures are very hard on my poor head." Actually she kept meticulous accounts of school records and later of the Bible women's meetings, pupils, salaries, and collections. Her monthly and annual reports were very detailed and complete.

She joked about her single blessedness. One day she announced that she had been invited to a tea that was only for those "not encumbered with husbands." It was always good for a laugh with her when she gave her address to someone. "I live with Mrs. Mary Coventry in the young ladies' household in Bulak," she would say pointedly, realizing that the other person knew she was nearly eighty years old.

She had a good time with young people, whoever they were.

During a furlough in 1911 she attended the meeting of the United Presbyterian General Assembly in Washington, Pennsylvania, and stayed with a friend of her seminary days. The family had moved to the town while Anna was a student and went to the Wednesday-evening prayer meeting at the church on their first opportunity. When the meeting closed, Anna made her way to the strangers and introduced herself, the first person to speak to them. A daughter in the family became a special friend and they corresponded regularly after Anna went to Egypt. After the friend married and children arrived, they too were remembered individually with their special interests. The whole family was delighted to entertain Miss Thompson during the Assembly, along with a pair of young ministers who were delegates. At first the young men were very respectful to the distinguished visitor from Egypt, but they soon learned that she enjoyed their fun and was willing to take some teasing herself. By the next day they learned that she could give as good as she got, and the fun was fast and furious, as the listening children remember to this day.

Some people find it hard to be at their best when they are traveling, especially if they are confined with a few persons for a long time in rather cramped conditions. But those who made the long journey back and forth between the United States and Egypt with Miss Anna Y found her a joy. One traveling companion wrote back home, "We wish that every party of missionaries might have our Miss Anna Y of rich experience in Christian service and joyous, youthful spirits" (she was sixty-nine years old at the time) "for we all owe much to her presence and cheer. And such a pilot to the field gives us, perhaps unconsciously, a better understanding of Egypt's need." Much of the time she stayed in her cabin, but the door was kept open and she received her visitors delightedly. One of her colleagues wrote to her once, "I am sure you will do the people good. One of your specialties is a kindly manner." She said herself that in this age of specialization her only specialty was people.

Miss Thompson's fantastic memory for faces and names was one of her greatest assets. Whenever she arrived at the Cairo railway station on one of her thousands of trips to greet or say farewell to missionaries and visitors, she spoke to the rough porters by name. They saluted the tall, quiet woman, always dressed in black or gray, as if she were the queen herself. She knew all the railway officials along the line up country and down, and at every station the window went down so she could call for her old friends and ask about their families. The story goes that Miss Anna Y disliked traveling by train in the United States because when the train stopped she found she didn't know a soul on the platform! Tram conductors and shopkeepers in every section of Cairo knew her, and she frequently knew their children's names. It was not uncommon for her to know the family connections in Egypt so well that she could tell people about relatives they did not know they had. An early colleague, in writing to *The United Presbyterian* in 1905, commented, "Without disparaging others, it may be said that Mrs. Harvey and her cousin, Miss Anna Thompson, surpass us all, so far as I know, in a certain knowledge of 'who's who.' That is, they have a marvelous knowledge and recollection of the near and distant relatives of their numerous native friends. Some of us have occasionally laughed at this genealogical folklore, but they have a distinct advantage in their ability to inquire of a woman intelligently concerning her 'sisters and cousins and aunts' in Alexandria, Assiut or elsewhere."

The students of the theological seminary lived in the Ezbekieh building for many years and were mothered by Mrs. Harvey and Miss Anna Y. They knew their personal problems and very often found a way to help. Some of the pastors speak gratefully of Miss Thompson's care when they were ill, and of her watchfulness for their health as well as for their spiritual needs. One of them said, "When she saw I was walking too fast she would tell me to slow down." This rather reverses the commonly held ideas of the two nationalities' characteristics!

It was well that Miss Anna Y enjoyed people so much, for she had the onerous task of looking after a great many of them. She was often at the hospitals to read to patients or simply to sit with them and show her sympathy. In the early years she found that many Egyptians felt it was a disgrace to be compelled to go into a hospital. They thought relatives should be able to care for them if they had any family feeling. Miss Thompson understood thoroughly their need for compassion in times of trial and illness. She quoted sympathetically the poor woman who had had much to bear, and who reached the climax of her story of woe by saying pathetically, "And there was no one to say to me, *'maalesh'* (never mind)."

Anna Thompson took on some surprising duties when she saw a need. One day, as she walked in the street with a young woman missionary, they caught up with a peasant woman who was having trouble balancing a large bundle of brush on her head. Miss Thompson stopped, put the load right, and then walked on without breaking the thread of her conversation. When the church needed cleaning, she went down and helped. When a single man staying temporarily at the mission needed some socks darned, she darned them. Her "odd jobs" were innumerable—house-hunting for a new missionary couple, helping Mrs. Harvey make grape juice for communion service, dusting the guest room before more visitors arrived—whatever had to be done, she tackled it. Her day's schedule sometimes read like this, "Up at five to get breakfast for the folks who were leaving, went to the train with them, looked after the washing"—and then off to begin her day's visiting and supervision of her helpers. Occasionally there is a brief note in the diary, "Nearly nervous today" or "Many guests. Very tired," but not often did she fall ill. She admitted to having lived on bread and milk for a week after an upset, but she did not stop work.

The new recruits in the mission were Miss Anna Y's special concern. Those who lived in the household said she would often slip into their room late in the evening to hear their Arabic lesson, practice the Arabic greetings, or tell them of her day's doings. She was very anxious for them to know the local customs so they would not ignorantly injure the sensibilities of the people they had come to serve. Sometimes on the very day of their arrival they would be claimed by Miss Thompson for a visit to one of the little schools she supervised. Walking through the dusty lanes, she would drill them on how they should greet the teacher. "Good morning, Miss Aziza," she would say over and over in Arabic, making a great point that the name must be used and correctly pronounced.

No one can remember Miss Anna Y being really angry, though sometimes she was hurt. She was not given to name calling, but one day she did say to the father of one of her Bible women, "You are an old lion." (He had been insisting that Miss Thompson give him the daughter's salary, which she steadfastly refused to do.) She hated gossip and would have no part in it. When a conversation seemed to be getting out of hand, she would break in with some utterly unrelated remark, such as "Mrs. Harvey gave me this scarf." That would surprise the group into silence and then into laughter. One day one of the mission wives launched into a long tirade about the outrageous behavior of her servant—one of many she'd had trouble with—and she finished by asking, "I don't think I'm hard to get along with, do you?" Miss Thompson was momentarily nonplussed. Just then the tea tray arrived and she said, not quite in response to the embarrassing question, "Our old Joe is a good cook." That became a favorite story in the mission family. When at times a change of subject was indicated, someone only needed to begin, "Our old Joe," and the group would burst into laughter.

One Thursday evening in the mission building Miss Thompson came into the room where a group had gathered for the weekly prayer meeting, and asked the leader if she might make an announcement before they began. She went to the front of the room, clasped her hands at her waist with a characteristic little lift of the shoulders, and said, "Rev. So-and-So has just gone to his reward," and then, after a slight pause, "or his accounting." Knowing the man and Miss Anna Y's opinion of him, the crowd had to laugh even at the news of a death. She was not above a critical judgment when she considered it was justified. After the bishop of Jerusalem had preached at the dedication of the new English church, she remarked that the sermon was "short and weak." Even Dr. Spurgeon failed to inspire her when she heard him in London—she said she'd heard better. In the privacy of her diary one night she wrote that one of the mission fathers had "prayed (?) for twenty minutes." She noted that the organist at church had played with "force and jollity" and that one of the teachers sang a solo at the Christian Endeavor meeting "dressed up like an Egyptian princess, eyebrows and all." A couple noted for their devotion to their cat came to call, and the diary says, "Mr. and Mrs. So-and-So and cat here for tea." At a hall where she went to hear a lecture her only reaction was, "Fine echoes!"

In the late 1920's an official visitor arrived in Egypt, ostensibly to inspect the work of his own organization—not the American mission. He became famous for his unerring instinct for mealtime in the various households. One evening he rang the bell just as the ladies in the Bulak household were gathering at the table. There was nothing to do but to invite him to join them, and another place was set. After supper the language students disappeared to their own apartment to study, leaving Miss Thompson to entertain the unexpected guest in her little sitting room. After an hour or so the bell rang in the girls' apartment and Miss Thompson called, "Won't you come down and join us?" Groaning at the thought of the next

day's assignments, they filed downstairs rather unhappily. The
conversation would have lagged if it had not been for the loquacity
of the visitor. Time passed, and the girls squirmed. Finally Miss Anna
Y rose to her feet. "Perhaps Mr. B. will lead us in prayer before he
leaves," she said, with a straight face. Surprised, he too got up,
prayed briefly, and took his departure. The girls gave Miss Anna Y
admiring grins and went back to their study.

The postman never missed Miss Thompson's door. Her correspondence was staggering. A gift was always acknowledged the
next day, and the letters poured out of her room. Her secret was
that she wrote briefly and shared the letters she received with other
people. One could be sure that a note to Anna Thompson would not
stop with her, unless it was something entirely personal and
confidential. Mutual friends kept track of each other with her as
go-between. Egyptian friends who had been sent to distant cities for
church or government work were not forgotten, and the church
people in the homeland were kept informed of the progress of the
work in Egypt. Sometimes she had to look after everybody else's
mail. After one short holiday she found a bundle of a hundred and
thirty-six packages waiting to be readdressed from the mission
building. During the war there would be long gaps in the mail
service, and then the letters would arrive by handfuls, to be eagerly
devoured. Even on sea voyages, when one would expect her to be
taking a well-earned rest, she kept at the writing, usually averaging
several letters every day.

Miss Thompson was a great collector of clippings. Her interest in
politics and social questions was intense. By the end of her life she
had filled a good-sized trunk with the newspaper and magazine
articles she had saved. Being able to read the Arabic papers with
more ease than most Westerners in Egypt, she knew the ins and outs
of the very involved local politics better than they. When she found
a person with similar knowledge to whom she could talk, a
conversation went on that would have astonished the Cairo cabinet
ministers. She knew many of the political leaders personally—
particularly those Coptic young men who had practiced their English
in her first Christian Endeavor Society—and she could read behind
the fine phrases to the realities of the situation. It was her custom,
even in her late seventies, to send the servant every week for the
Egyptian "funny papers"—comic magazines on topical subjects with
outrageous cartoons and captions in colloquial Arabic. Some of her

C. E. boys of the early years appeared in these cartoons rather frequently. She shook her head over some of their lampooned shenanigans, but she found the colloquial captions (words not usually transcribed into the formal, written Arabic) extremely funny.

The mission building was a fine vantage point from which to watch the political life of the people. From that balcony she and many others viewed the great parades for Saad Zaghlul and demonstrations for independence. These got out of hand sometimes and there was bloodshed in the streets. Frequently Miss Anna Y was caught in such disturbances and would find herself a long way from home without any hope of finding a tram, taxi, or carriage. This did not seem to dismay her, but it resulted in some very long walks. She reported that she just "stood here and there for an hour or so." She was in the dentist's chair when bombs were dropped on Cairo, "apparently by a hostile machine," as she said. No one ever saw her panic. Sometimes she even seemed to invite injury. Going through one of the badly policed parts of the city with a nervous young companion on her way to a little school, she was blocked by a large crowd of angry, fighting men. The usual mob of partisans had joined in, supposedly separating the antagonists, but actually adding to the uproar. Miss Thompson, frail and stooped by this time, waded into the crowd. Going right to the center of the fight, she touched one of the men on the shoulder and said, "Friend, you must not do this." Astonished, he dropped his fists, and the fight was over.

Miss Anna Y was a strange mixture of formality and the opposite. She retained the long skirts and long sleeves of her youth, and the skirts were a real hazard on Egypt's dusty lanes and streets. One day, as she and Miss Smith were plodding up the steps after a morning's visiting, Miss Thompson remarked that the stairs needed sweeping. Miss Smith, a little tartly, said, "That's strange since you sweep them every day with your skirt." If one of the young ladies in the house happened to yawn, Miss Thompson sent her straight off to put on more clothing, particularly to cover her arms, not because she was shocked by short sleeves, but because she was sure the girl was going to take cold. These younger workers always appreciated the fact that Miss Anna Y never reminded them that their lot was much easier than the life the pioneer missionaries had known.

It was puzzling to the younger members of the household that though they were on first-name or even nickname basis with

everyone else, each was always addressed as "Miss" by Anna
Thompson. More than that, she usually called her own cousin "Mrs.
Harvey," even in her diary, to the end of her life, though they had
lived together so many years.

In other ways Miss Anna Y did not stand on ceremony. On one
memorable day she took a foreign visitor to see the girls' school
where she had been headmistress for so long. The girls were in the
chapel and the program had begun. Miss Thompson, leading her
guest, moved confidently up the aisle, expecting the missionary in
charge to pause and let her introduce the visitor. She, in her turn,
expected Miss Thompson to see that she could not interrupt the
chapel service. Miss Thompson kept advancing, but the program
went on. Finally Miss Thompson realized she was not going to be
recognized and she was forced to retreat. She went home very
shaken and perplexed, not because she was not allowed to speak, but
because her guest had not been welcomed suitably. The missionary
in charge was even more astonished that Miss Thompson would
think of breaking into the chapel service. The gap in the generations
was very obvious that day.

More than once Miss Anna Y asked to be allowed to step down
from an important assignment and take on something much less in
the public eye, so that a younger person might replace her. She
quietly accepted the fact that the men were running the mission in
the early years. But when it was proposed that the men be permitted
to attend the women's own little society, she objected. She said she
would agree only on condition that all would work toward full
representation of the women in the official association. It was tiny
Miss Smith who took a small stool, marched into the closed meeting
of the men during association sessions, sat down, and refused to be
stared out of countenance. From then on the women had a part in
those deliberations, which affected them so intimately. The association minutes previous to that time include meek requests for
furloughs—frequently overdue—and joint requests from Miss Thompson and Miss Smith for a helper to be assigned to them. Usually a
later minute reports that the men had sent the new recruit
elsewhere! One of the Egyptian churchmen made the remark that if
women were present when the Holy Spirit was given, they must have
been in another room. This was one remark that really vexed Miss
Anna Y. But she advised one of the young pastors that in a family
quarrel he would usually find that it was the woman who was to
blame.

She was much concerned when one of the mission staff decided that his views had changed and he must become a Plymouth Brother. She happened to be in a train returning from upcountry when, looking out of the window at a station in the hope of seeing the local pastor, she saw instead this former United Presbyterian missionary. He had been visiting "some of the disaffected members" of the church. She said her heart sank and she wondered what she ought to do. Egyptian-like, she said (she thought), "O Lord, what is my sin that I should be faced with him?" But when he came on board, she plucked up her courage and spoke to him. He asked for news about a number of people from home. She said it was obvious he wasn't hearing often from America. He said he did not take USA papers. She came back at him with, "Is it wrong to take papers?" With that a day-long discussion began, arguing about church government and Plymouth Brethren doctrines. She asked him to read the New Testament again, praying for direction and holding the idea that maybe he had been mistaken in the change he had made. She asked him why he had not gone up the Nile as he had intended. He replied that he had finished the work he came to do. Miss Thompson's inner comment was, "He doesn't know that I think he's leaving Egypt in answer to prayer!"

It is amusing to read Miss Anna Y's description of a visiting missionary on her way home from China—"She fills all one's former idea of a real missionary: tall, thin, energetic and a little careless about fashion." There were times when Anna herself had felt that she must perforce be careless about fashion. In her late twenties she was invited to a fashionable British wedding, but she called on the hostess and told her, "Unless I can wear my black silk dress I can't go, since I can't afford to buy a new one." She did indulge in new gloves and a fichu with pink ribbons, and attended the wedding wearing "Mrs. Watson's hat with my feather on it." When a new coat was imperative, she could find only one in the city that was large enough for her, and she was horrified that she had to pay the shocking sum of twenty dollars for it. Occasionally in the record of her middle years there is mention of ripping up a blouse for renovations, or dyeing an old skirt. There was no great need for such economics, as the supporting societies at home tried to send her gifts for personal needs. When they learned it was useless to send Anna Thompson money for herself, they sent materials. Once during a furlough the ladies wanted her to look nice for a public appearance

and presented her with a whole new outfit. To their dismay she
appeared in her old clothes, saying that a missionary oughtn't to
look so fashionable! In her late seventies, when she was living in the
Bulak house, one of the language students went to her room on an
errand, but stopped in blank amazement when she saw that Miss
Thompson was carefully darning a handkerchief. This was so far
outside the range of her own economies that she completely forgot
what she had come for.

No one will ever know where all of Miss Anna Y's money went. A
great deal of it went into scholarships for her pupils, help for needy
Bible women and their relatives, and especially for support of the
churches. It was the custom for a congregation preparing to build a
church to pass around a paper among the mission staff for pledges.
At one meeting of the association three such papers had already
made the rounds when an appeal came for a much needed bell for a
recently completed church. (Obviously one needs a bell if he does
not own a clock.) Miss Thompson approved of the request because
the congregation itself had given sacrificially to pay for the church
building, but she thought it would be poor policy to present a fourth
subscription paper just then. Instead, she suggested that one of the
missionary societies designate a part of its thank offering for the
bell. This was done, to the delight of the givers and the receivers. On
one occasion a collecting committee came to Miss Anna Y, saying
that they had put her name at the head of the paper. When she
looked at the amount they had put beside her name, she was
startled, as it was considerably more than she had expected to
contribute to that particular cause, but she let it stand. During the
last days of her life one of the visitors who was admitted to her
hospital room arrived with a request for a gift of this sort. She did
not consider this bad taste, but welcomed him and promised there
would be something for his church, sending him away with her
prayers for his success.

Miss Thompson kept nothing entirely for herself. Whoever was on
hand when a gift package was delivered, immediately became a
sharer in the largess. But she had a following of local beggars who
sometimes almost drove her distracted. The servant would try to
send some villainous-looking person away from the door, only to be
told that he was Miss Thompson's friend, and the lady herself,
coming on the scene, would admit this was true and welcome him in.
She would listen to his latest, most preposterous tale, reach into the

deep pocket in her voluminous skirt, which always held a supply of silver, and slip something into his hand with a murmur of advice. Meanwhile the servant would stand guard, looking daggers at the man, and disapproving heartily of what his respected Miss Thompson was doing. When the rest of the household joined in the chorus, she would sigh and agree.

"Yes, I know he may use the money to buy hashish. But he may also be hungry," she would say.

One day she came away from the telephone with a very bemused look. "Can you imagine?" she asked. "That was old Sayyid asking me to pray for him over the telephone!" Some of the begging notes to the too generous missionary have survived—they fall out of all sorts of unlikely places among her papers. One reads, "Respected Miss Thompson: We have no food and the children are very hungry. I hope you can help us and I ask the Lord to keep you." She would certainly not have been able to resist such a plea.

One of Miss Anna Y's regular "friends" was the occasion of her having to go to court. He had been persuaded—or bribed—to accuse a prominent Muslim convert of having insulted Islam in a public address. The convert was arrested and thrown into jail. The whole mission was up in arms, demanding that the law of freedom of religion be complied with, since there had been no such insult. Miss Thompson was called to the hearing as a witness and had the unpleasant task of proving that her begging friend was "a liar and deceiver, who can make a beautiful prayer." She said she had had great hope that the poor wretched man would himself be converted. Some people were sure that he was a drug addict and Miss Anna Y said, "I have a few other friends somewhat like him!" During the court session the judge, a Muslim, asked Miss Thompson why the missionaries taught religion at the Girls' College. She gave him the reasons and he replied, "This is a prophet and this is a prophet. They are the same to me." Miss Thompson retorted, "They are not the same to me. If I believe that Christ died for me, should I not tell it?" and that ended the passage at arms. Some of the mission men had tried to arrange for Miss Thompson to be excused from appearing at court, thinking she might be harassed and embarrassed, but they need not have been concerned.

Though Anna had her reticences, she was not at all prudish. During her long years in Egypt she absorbed the local habit of calling a spade a spade, not bothering with any overly polite circumlocutions. One evening in a small meeting she was discussing a situation that had come up and was being candid as usual. In the midst of it her eye caught the shocked expression on the face of a British soldier in the group. He was staring at her incredulously. She interrupted herself long enough to say, "To the pure all things are pure," and went right on. When a scandal occurred involving one of her younger workers, she did not disown the girl but arranged for one of the missionaries to marry the lovers. She paid for the bride's outfit from her own pocket. She was very grieved because the gossip cast a shadow on the home of a Muslim convert as well as damaging the reputation of her corps of helpers.

There is a teasing letter from her old friend Miss Johnston among Anna's papers. It was written during a furlough when Miss Johnston had talked with Anna's father. She said he inquired whether his daughter was drinking tea and coffee. When she replied that Anna took them "only in moderation," he did not seem to be too shocked. Then the letter went on to hint at some young man's interest in Anna, but that apparently was not serious.

There is one saddening chapter in Miss Thompson's life she never talked about after it was over. That was her engagement to marry Dr. Gulian Lansing. He was of course older than she and he had been widowed twice. His first wife had died in a cholera epidemic along with their year-old child. He married Miss Dales of the mission in 1866 and she became Miss Anna Y's great friend. She too died, in 1889, and Anna was with her, closing her eyes when the end came. It is uncertain when Dr. Lansing began to think about Anna as a possible wife. They had been colleagues for many years, from the day of her arrival in Cairo in 1871, and particularly during her years as headmistress of the Ezbekieh school when he went every day for the morning devotions and Bible classes. He was a man of deep faith, who sometimes moved ahead with the business of the mission when the needed financial support was not in sight. He was a person whose judgment was much respected, as well as a great Hebrew scholar.

Evidence indicates that Miss Anna Y agreed to marry him not long before her furlough in 1890. She was due to return to the field about the same time as her prospective bridegroom, but the other missionaries considered it improper for an engaged couple to travel on the same boat, no matter how well chaperoned, so he took an early boat and she followed a little later. By the time she reached Egypt, real trouble was brewing. Some of the mission fathers thought it would shock the Egyptians, especially Orthodox Copts, if a man had three wives during his lifetime. They had convinced Dr. Thompson that his daughter would be harming the work if she went ahead with her plans. She was a mature woman with experience in Egypt, which he did not have, but he was her father and she would not go on without his blessing. So the engagement was broken and the wedding dress, ready for the ceremony, was destroyed or given away—no one knows what happened to it. Anna concealed her private grief and took up the thread of her work again. If she felt sorry for herself, there was no outward sign, nor was there any resentment against her father or the people who had taken it upon themselves to interfere. But the dream died hard.

One afternoon, several years later, she was preparing to go out calling with one of the other single women when the latter asked her to wait a moment as she had something to tell her. Her news was that one of the men of the staff, who had lost his wife some time previously, had asked her to marry him, and she had agreed. Miss Thompson was startled. She seemed unable to respond, and catching up her hat and literature, she suddenly left the room. Probably no calls were made *that* afternoon. Several hours later she returned and apologized to her colleague for her abrupt departure. Memories of her own disappointment had been too much for her. She said she hoped her own experience would not be repeated, and then she added, "Be sure. Then go ahead as you are led." From then on she took a deep interest in the details of the wedding plans and helped the bride decide on the furnishings of the new home.

When Miss Anna Y was in her late seventies, an unexpected caller appeared at the house, asking for her. He introduced himself as a relative of Dr. Lansing, and said that he had been in missionary work in the Cameroun and was passing through the city. Someone had told him that Miss Thompson had known his relative well and could give him information about his life in Egypt. Miss Anna Y welcomed him, kept him for lunch, and talked freely about Dr. Lansing's missionary career. But at tea time one of the young ladies surprised her as she was standing by the window with a faraway, sad expression on her face. When she went up to her with an inquiring look, Miss Thompson said pathetically, "He took the last picture I had of Dr. Lansing." The other was indignant. "Why in the world did you let him have it?" she demanded. Miss Thompson sighed. "He asked for it," she said simply—and that was all anyone needed to do if he wanted anything Miss Anna Y had.

The veteran missionary finally had to give up the strenuous walking and stair-climbing of her youth. She began to depend more and more on public transport or the cars of generous friends. Her old friends were slipping away. Mrs. Harvey had passed her eighty-second birthday when the pioneer missionary Dr. John Giffen died. Miss Thompson wrote that at his funeral "the five *old* ladies sat in one seat," but one of the five was gone in less than two months. Mrs. Harvey later took ill and was in the hospital for several months. Miss Anna Y visited her every day and carried on the work of the house and her mission assignments as well. Eventually Mrs. Harvey was able to return home, but she required a great deal of care. Anna rescued her when she "tumbled herself out of bed," read to her, and sat with her at night when it was necessary. One Sunday evening, after Dr. Charles Watson had preached at the English service, Mrs. Harvey sent for him to come up to the apartment. She said, "Come and finish your sermon here. Here there are nothing but a lot of women who don't know anything!"

This cousin and dear friend of Anna died in her eighty-ninth year and the home was broken up. This made it necessary for Miss Thompson to leave the Ezbekieh building where she had lived for fifty-one years, almost all of that time in the same room. The move must have been a great wrench for her but she soon made a place for herself in the Bulak household. (A few years after Miss Thompson's death the Bulak residence was turned over to British missionaries and they conducted a formal dedication service, complete with bell, book, and incense. As they began their ritual in Miss Thompson's former room, some of the American missionaries who were trailing along in the procession admitted to feeling a little provoked. They said later that Miss Anna Y's prayers had consecrated that room far more than anyone else's poor power to add or detract.)

There was a great celebration on the occasion of the fiftieth anniversary of the arrival of Miss Smith and Miss Thompson in Egypt. Each received a sheaf of fifty white roses. Crowds poured through the house to bring their congratulations. It was slightly premature for Miss Smith, since she had arrived a few months later than Miss Thompson, but it seemed appropriate to honor them together. Nine years later there was another big celebration for Miss Thompson's eightieth birthday. This time there were two bouquets of eighty dark-red roses and a huge cake, besides almost sixty other bouquets, making the house look like a flower garden. It had been planned as a surprise, but as soon as the invitations went out, letters and telegrams began to arrive, and the secret was out. A poem written in her honor that day contained these lines:

> God gave you powers renewed for all these years,
> And you have given back your golden life;
> He gave you courage, quieted your fears,
> And filled your heart with peace in Egypt's strife.
> Have you demanded comfort, ease or rest,
> Or quailed a moment through these numbered days?
> You shame us all with selfless life well blessed
> While friends unnumbered sing your well-earned praise.
> But you, by living, praise but God above;
> Your service here reflects His perfect love.

One of the people present said it was wonderful to see her as she stood or sat through the hours, happy but with complete dignity. She recognized her visitors of every nationality as they greeted her and made some appropriate response. There was no doubt that Anna Thompson was able to carry off any situation. She went in to dinner one night on the arm of Lord Kitchener, and on the next night she sat on the mud floor in a poor home and ate her dinner with her fingers from a tray, completely at ease in both cases. In spite of everything, she told a reporter at the birthday party that her life had been "uneventful though very, very happy."

When Miss Thompson and Miss Smith reached their seventies, there began to be a great deal of correspondence from the foreign and women's boards on the subject of pensions and retirements. Alarmed people in the Egyptian churches wrote passionate letters to the women's board, pleading that these two elderly missionaries be allowed to stay on in the field. The board replied that the doughty pioneers would be allowed to make their own choices about their retirement years. As it turned out, this was one time when they completely disagreed. Miss Smith's eyesight was very bad and she felt she was growing to be a burden, so without any fuss she made her plans to sail for home. She had a big send-off at the Cairo railway station. A crowd of schoolgirls in white dresses, carrying bouquets, started to sing. One after another they broke down until at last the song dissolved into sobs. But, as Miss Anna Y remarked

later, "Miss Smith was calm." With her arms full of flowers and a
gentle smile on her face, she steamed out of the old station which
she had seen so often, and began her long journey home.

Miss Thompson had foregone her last furlough because she was
determined that she would die in Egypt and be buried with the
people she had loved and served so long. Her health remained fairly
good and she got out often, with Mrs. Coventry at the wheel of the
faithful Ford. The noon prayer meeting at the mission building in
Ezbekieh nearly always found her in her chair. On her way by taxi
to make a speech in one of the suburbs she received a bad jolt and
her back was injured. She managed to keep the appointment but she
felt the effects of the accident for some time. Three days after
saying farewell to Miss Smith she was confined to bed with what the
doctors called muscular rheumatism in her back, and after a few
more days she was moved to the German Deaconess' Hospital. It was
her very first experience as a patient in a hospital. (That particular
hospital had begun as an idea in the mind of a German pastor and
Dr. Lansing. It opened in 1885, with Dr. Lansing as chairman of the
governing committee.) The deaconesses were very kind to Miss
Thompson, and twenty years later some of them still spoke of her
with affection and some awe.

The room across the hall from Miss Anna Y was occupied by a
prominent judge in the Mixed Courts. One day he asked to be
wheeled over to Miss Thompson's room. As he entered, he said, "I
have come to call on Saint Anna." She had many callers from the
great and the unknown, the rich and the poor. Mrs. Coventry was
there every day until illness forced her to enter a hospital herself.
After a few weeks Miss Thompson was allowed to go home, but once
again the rheumatism became unbearable, this time in her hands.
Another month in the hospital, home again for three months, then
the final ambulance ride and three weary months of pain before the
tired spirit was released. She took comfort from her visitors and her
letters. Some of the mission staff visited her morning and afternoon,
reading her mail to her and answering it as she directed them. Often
there were some of her Bible women and other Egyptian women
friends sitting quietly on the floor in her room, simply keeping her
company and knowing they didn't need to talk to their beloved Sitt
Thompson. The Egyptian pastor came frequently, and twice he held
communion services for her there in the hospital room. She kept
very cheerful in spite of weakness and much pain.

Some of her old begging friends insisted on seeing her. The doctors finally forbade their admittance, as it was too tiring for her. But persistent ones found the back stairs and sometimes were able to elude the hospital attendants and reach her room. One day this happened while one of the men of the mission was calling on Miss Thompson. She asked the missionary to go with the man and give him a small amount of money for her. Very unwillingly he did as she asked. When he had left the hospital, the beggar slipped back in and told her that he had not been given the money. When the story came out, the missionary was so exasperated that he put very strict injunctions on the hospital staff to keep such persons out of the building by any means necessary.

Miss Thompson grew gradually weaker. One day she remembered that the younger missionary sitting with her had come from Oregon. Motioning her to come close, Miss Anna Y feebly sang a strange little song, and asked whether her visitor recognized it, but she did not. "An Indian chief taught me that song in Oregon," Miss Thompson said.

When she heard there was to be a large inter-mission meeting in the city in a few days' time, she was delighted. She said, "I will die on Thursday night, so the funeral will be on Friday. The visitors will still be here from all over Egypt, and since Friday is the government holiday, the friends here will be free to come too." And it happened just that way. She went to her heavenly home on December 15, 1932, a Thursday. The funeral she had foreseen was a very large one, filling the big church in Ezbekieh to its capacity. At her grave great men and women from East and West stood with the humble and uncultured, old and young.

Miss Anna Y kept a diary as long as she could handle a pen, some pages bearing mute testimony to the agony that the effort was costing her. She wrote of happy visits with old friends, of the progress of a new congregation in Cairo, of the visit from the man who needed money to put the roof on a new church, and of the group who came to take communion with her. A scrap of blotting paper marks the place where the writing ceased. Most appropriately the record stops in the middle of a sentence, with a comma. For the story was not finished, nor will it ever be finished, either in the land of Egypt or in God's eternity.

INDEX